MATTHEW

Other Highland Books

MATTHEW

Bob Jackson

HIGHLAND BOOKS

Printed in Great Britain for
HIGHLAND BOOKS
Broadway House, The Broadway,
Crowborough, East Sussex TN6 1BY
by Richard Clay Ltd, Bungay, Suffolk
Typeset by CST, Eastbourne, East Sussex

For Matthew
If you had not been so wonderfully special,
I would have had nothing to say.

CONTENTS

PREFACE

This book has been produced jointly by my wife, Christine, and myself. Much of the material is either based on her notes and diary or is the result of discussion between us. I am simply the one who has written it down in book form. It was not just that I needed the support of Christine for writing: the story itself is our joint offering.

I have written my account at the most months and at the least hours away from the events described; not from the calm detachment of elapsed years, but from the immediacy of battling with the crisis itself. I hope you will find this a strength rather than a weakness.

I have not attempted to write a textbook for the bereaved, but rather to tell the story of how God has dealt with us. The experience of other bereaved people will, no doubt, be different. What I have tried to do is to share our perspective on the reality of God, the power of resurrection faith and the joy of heaven; and I hope that reading our story will make you sing more than it makes you cry.

1
Gift of God

As I watched from the maternity block window, the rockets scattered their stars over Ashford as bonfire night drew to a close and my wife Christine came to the end of a long and difficult labour. The staff had ejected me from the delivery room when things had got tricky and I was having an anxious time of waiting. The doctor kept coming out to telephone for reinforcements and advice.

'There's nothing tragic or anything,' he said. 'It's just tricky.'

Finally, I saw our newborn son, Matthew, trundled down the corridor. He was still bloody, but beautiful. It was a wonderful feeling to be a dad.

We had been married for just over two years. Christine had taught geography in secondary schools, first in Kirkby, near Liverpool, and then, after our marriage, in Hammersmith. I was an economist, advising civil servants and ministers in the Departments of Transport and Environment in Westminster. I enjoyed this enormously, especially when advising on railway policy, as I was still a train-spotter at heart. We had both been Christians from our teenage years, and our local church was as important to us as were our jobs. We were members of a small but growing Baptist church in Ashford, Middlesex. We were Anglicans at heart, but the Baptist church had become the right one for us during our years in Ashford. Matthew's early years were spent in the warmth of that fellowship. He grew up fast— conversing in sentences before most children had learnt to say 'mum', and keeping us on our toes with his constant chatter and questions.

Towards the end of our time in Ashford I was back in the maternity block, this time staying in for the whole of the delivery. So I was able to hold Ruth when she was just a few seconds old, and marvel at the expertise with which she promptly stuck her thumb in her mouth. Our family, so it seemed, was complete.

Soon after Ruth was born, I became a student again. We had felt for a couple of years that God was calling us to full-time ministry and I had been accepted by a Church of England selection conference. The first inkling of this call had come before Matthew's birth. When I had mentioned this to Christine she had said, 'I've always wanted to be a vicar's wife.' This had floored me for a while as it had seemed quite a strange ambition! But then I'd wondered whether that had been God's way of preparing Christine for the future. We had tested out the call by going about things in a way calculated to invite rejection. I had written to our very 'churchy' bishop, who'd done his best to put this Baptist off, but had just failed to do so. Our conviction that God was calling us to the Church of England had matured over the next couple of years, and so, with our young family, we had moved to St John's College, Nottingham, to begin our training.

After three happy years at St John's it was time to move again. We returned to my home city of Sheffield where I became curate of Christ Church, Fulwood. Christine was a Lancashire lass but had had a desire to live in Sheffield even before she'd known me—an ambition she could no more explain than her desire to be a vicar's wife. She had even cried when leaving Sheffield after visiting my family—so strong had been her feelings about the place.

Matthew seemed an exceptional child—bright and forward, good-looking and outgoing, with a wonderful sense of fun and humour. There was a particular attractiveness about him that marked him out as special. His qualities of gentleness and consideration, together with his capacity to enjoy life, made him especially loved by his friends and his teachers. He was always top of the class at school and clearly overflowed with ability and promise.

But there was one cloud on our horizon dating back to before Matthew's birth.

Christine, when expecting Matthew, had a threatened miscarriage. The doctor kept her in bed for a few days and things sorted themselves out. During that time she had a strong sense that God was speaking to her. I was at home with 'flu at the time and rather resented running up and down stairs for someone who looked outwardly fit and well. But Christine called me to the bedside and told me, with some hesitation, three things she believed God had said.

'I'm not going to lose the baby—it'll be born all right,' was the first. I was happy to accept that. Indeed I had always been confident of it. But Christine had been offering her baby to God if only it could be born safely—as Hannah had offered her son Samuel in the Old Testament.

'It's going to be a boy,' was her second conviction. My family produced far more girls than boys; nevertheless we then and there settled on a name—Matthew, which means 'Gift of God'.

'What's the third thing?' I asked.

'That we won't have him for ever. One day we'll lose him,' she said, watching my face carefully as I stood at the foot of the bed. My natural reaction would have been to dismiss this as the imaginings of a pregnant female. But a sense of awe overrode that reaction.

'I don't know, perhaps you're right, but whatever that means it's a long way in the future,' I replied, trying not to appear too concerned. But underneath I had a terrible feeling that Christine was right . . .

Over the months and years we both tried to qualify or minimise, for each other's sake, what Christine believed God had told her. We said to each other that if he were to die before us, Matthew would at least be an adult and have achieved something remarkable.

'Perhaps,' I said to Christine one day, 'it was a warning that we'll lose him like Bob and Doris are losing Margaret.' (Margaret was the daughter of friends of ours who was going overseas as a missionary teacher.) Or perhaps—I told myself at times—we were wrong and it would never happen at all. Most of the time we put the matter to the back of our minds, keeping our feelings to ourselves, and concentrated on bringing up Matthew and Ruth to be happy and normal children. And this, for the most part, we succeeded in doing.

We had many friends in our close-knit Baptist church in Ashford and some of them, like ourselves, did not disapprove of infant baptism as the denomination officially does. For one such couple, Ros and Ian, we became Godparents to their new son Andrew. Andrew had appeared a chesty child since birth, at three months cystic fibrosis was diagnosed and so his long-term outlook was not good. However, Ros was a nurse and with expert care at home Andrew progressed quite well for his first few years. Shortly after we left Ashford, his condition began to deteriorate. He contracted a viral chest infection and began to require even more attention. One Christmas Andrew went into hospital a very ill child, but after much prayer, both from the church and many Christians in other fellowships he became well enough to go home, only to return again within a few weeks. This time, despite much prayer, Andrew went to his heavenly Father.

It was a tragic experience for us all, but the Lord showed his love and concern for Ros and Ian by blessing them, and one or two others in Ashford, with several beautiful visions which assured them and us of Andrew's place in heaven. The joy of that certainty was reflected in the very moving and triumphant funeral service. After this, we thought more seriously about God's word (if that is what it was) to Christine, and decided that just as Jesus was God's gift to the world, so Matthew was God's gift to us; but along with the precious gift, we had been given a speck of myrrh. Like Mary we kept all these things in our hearts—not wanting to risk anything getting back to Matthew himself. Just as Mary had lived with the burden of the myrrh signifying her son's death so Christine and I lived with the belief that we would outlive Matthew.

Nevertheless, with these things stored at the back of our minds, we had happy years watching Matthew and Ruth growing up. The years at Nottingham and Christ Church, Fulwood, were full, rich and rewarding.

When Matthew was eight, we moved to another parish in Sheffield—St Mark's Grenoside —where I was made vicar. Christine's teenage dream of being a vicar's wife in Sheffield had finally been realised.

Matthew was now a sturdy ten year old. He and I shared a love of trains and of a model railway that ran from his bedroom to ours through a tunnel in the wall; of football in general and Sheffield Wednesday in particular; and of hill-walking. We had a holiday house in Llanberis in North Wales and became experts on the narrow gauge steam railways and at climbing Snowdon. Matthew was a keen observer of all things mechanical, which he would translate into model form with his 'Lego' when we got back home. Whether it was the cliff railway at Lynton or the trams at Crich, a replica would appear in his bed-room a few days after a visit or holiday. He enjoyed bird-watching, too, and became the family expert at identifying species; and he loved music, becoming proficient on the piano. At Grenoside he became an enthusiastic member of the St John Ambulance Cadets—and liked to tie us up in slings and bandages!

At the heart of what we shared with Matthew was our Christian faith. From the time of his earliest words, Matthew had always expressed a faith in Jesus—one which he had learned from us, our friends and our church fellowships. He came out with all the usual theological questions that children ask, but years earlier than one would have expected: 'Who made God?' he asked and dealt with before his fourth birthday!

He was particularly interested in heaven. He asked me, 'Will there be model railways in heaven, Dad?' I took care to answer positively, 'Of course there will be, but much better layouts than ours. Or if not model railways, something even better.' We wanted to give Matthew a positive and concrete picture of heaven: he might be there before us; besides I could see the damage done by parents who gave their children a dull or inadequate picture. Such a picture could well stick with them for life and colour the whole of their Christian faith.

Matthew would store up his hardest questions, in his pre-school years, for Christine on a Sunday evening when I was out taking a church service. Baby Ruth would be tucked up in her cot and Matthew would settle down on the settee with Christine.

'How do we know the way to heaven, Mummy?' he asked when he was three. 'We can't catch a train to get there.' Christine answered, 'You don't have to worry about getting there. Being sure you love Jesus is what matters and he's the way to get there. It's like when you catch a train—you can trust the train to get you where you want to go and you don't have to worry about it yourself.' Matthew chewed this over for a moment. Then he said, 'When we go there you two can walk, but Jesus will carry me.'

When we moved to Nottingham he and Ruth were baptised together in the chapel at St John's College. Matthew was three at the time and we explained to him what the ceremony was about: it was to show that he was one of Jesus' friends; that Jesus had washed him clean of the naughty things he had done; and that he would have a life with Jesus for ever. He kept a bearing of remarkable seriousness throughout the service. At the point of baptism he stood on a chair and bent his head over the font. It was a special moment for all who were there. Being articulate well beyond his years Matthew was able to express both a faith of his own and an understanding of the meaning of baptism. We all had the sense that, though we had observed a delayed infant baptism, we had actually witnessed a very special believer's baptism.

'Why were you staring into the water so hard?' we asked when we got home. He replied, 'I was watching all the black spots in the water.' As there were no black spots seen by anyone else, we wondered what it was that God had been saying to him in that special moment.

About three years later, during my curacy at Fulwood, we had a 'hunger lunch' after the Sunday morning service to remind us of how little those in the poor countries of the world had to eat. After lunch, Peter Jenkins, an old boyhood friend of mine who was the local representative for Tear Fund—a Christian relief and development agency that tries to meet spiritual and physical needs in the Third World—showed a filmstrip about the organisation's work. Watching this, Matthew's concentration never wavered. He was deeply moved by what he saw and took away a collecting box. From this time onwards, he developed a keen sense of the injustice in the world and an impatience with politicians who did nothing about it.

He was always interested in the news on television and became frustrated when the politicians failed to pursue what to him were the obvious answers to world poverty and inequality. He asked, as we watched the coverage of the famine in Ethiopia, 'Isn't there enough food in the world to go round, Mum?'

'Well, yes, Matthew, there is. But a lot of it is stored up by rich countries like ours and it's mostly for sale, not to give away.'

'But that's stupid—if we've got the food we should give it to them. It's obvious!'

Matthew, it seemed, had both a trust in Jesus and a concern for God's world that were his own—not something he put on to please us.

In June 1985 Mission England came to Sheffield with Billy Graham speaking for eight nights at Bramhall Lane, Sheffield United's football ground. Matthew was cross that he hadn't come to Hillsborough, Sheffield Wednesday's home just down the hill from Grenoside, but he, like the rest of us, joined in enthusiastically. Our church took many people to hear Billy Graham and a number went forward in response to his appeal. The Friday night crowd formed the largest evangelistic meeting in Britain for twenty years, and 6,092 people went forward in response to Billy Graham's appeal. The first on the pitch by several yards was one of my own church wardens. Several of the others who had come with us also responded.

Matthew and Ruth both went forward that night too, although we had given them no special encouragement. Billy Graham spoke about the dangers of neutrality: 'Jesus never allows you to be neutral about him. There are two roads, two masters, two destinies, and you have to make the choice.' Our children were sitting with their cousins —the children of my sister, Sue—about four rows behind us, high in the splendid new stand behind the podium. First Ruth came past us, typically calm and matter of fact, then Matthew, full of emotion, his face streaming with tears but unembarrassed about them. Out of all the thousands of people on the football pitch, Matthew's counsellor turned out to be an old friend from Fulwood—Irene Davis. She took Matthew through the literature prepared for children and made sure he knew what he was doing in wanting to give his life and destiny to Jesus. Several counsellors told us how moved they had been by the impact which the evening had clearly made on Matthew. And so we climbed back to the stand to meet the rest of our party as the setting sun silhouetted the city skyline around the brightly floodlit green of the slowly emptying pitch.

When we got home, the four of us prayed together at midnight with a new sense of equality as a truly Christian family. Matthew's Bible was fairly well worn but after that it was read more regularly, and he began to pray more readily and with greater conviction. Three weeks later he wrote to Irene:

Dear Mrs. Davis,
Thank you for writing to me. I'm sorry I'm such a long time writing back. Things have been busy. I am trying to read the Gospels and letters of the New Testament every day. I have found a lot out about God, heaven, and parables. We go on holiday to Wales and Llanberis a week on Wednesday. School finishes the following Friday. I am going to take my Bible and finish Matthew and Mark and start on John. We are taking our grand-parents with us. I hope you have a nice holiday and keep well. I keep hoping John John will come to Hillsborough.

Yours sincerely,
Matthew Jackson

John John was an evangelist whom Matthew had known at St John's college.

At our holiday home in Llanberis, on Sundays we had our own family services in which the children took part. From this time on, Matthew insisted on doing the talks, which he would spend time the previous day preparing—and an excellent preacher he turned out to be, modelling himself on the family service talks in church!

He was certainly living up to his name—Gift of God.

2
Suddenly One Afternoon

The summer after Mission Sheffield we went to Austria for a family holiday. We went earlier than usual, partly because it was cheaper than in high season but also because St Mark's was due to have a curate for the first time and I didn't want to abandon him too soon after his ordination. By our standards the holiday was expensive and we had spent the winter saving for it. Though looking forward to going, we were not completely carefree. Christine, particularly, felt slightly uneasy, despite praying about the holiday and finding no good reason for not going. We spent a few days with our old friends in Ashford, taking time to do some sightseeing in London. Then we flew to Austria to begin a two week holiday in Mayrhofen, a small holiday town nestling among high mountains in the Tyrol.

The holiday was wonderful! Matthew enjoyed the Austrian food to the full, starting with a Sunday lunch consisting entirely of a giant ice-cream concoction called a *fruchtbecher*.

'That's the best Sunday lunch I've even had, Mum,' he concluded. He loved the *Zillertalbahn*— the narrow gauge railway that runs down the Ziller valley from Mayrhofen to the junction with the main line at Jenbach. On the Monday we caught a steam train down to Jenbach to do some train-spotting and Matthew spent the trip out on the old-fashioned balcony at the end of the last coach.

'Come on out, Mum. It's much better out here!' he shouted excitedly at a reluctant Christine. 'Oh, come on, you'll enjoy it!' Christine obeyed and Matthew exclaimed, 'See, it's great. You can feel all the vibrations of the coach. You can see the track underneath you. You can wave at everyone. You can smell the smoke. You can see the engine round the curves! It's great!' His enjoyment overwhelmed us all.

Our holiday proceeded with a mixture of train trips and cable-car rides, and—on the days we were saving money—alpine walks. We also played crazy golf and, in the evenings, solo whist at the hotel. The World Cup was just beginning, and the hotel owner brought out a television so that Matthew and I could follow the fortunes of the British teams. Those were lovely and precious family days together after months of intense busy-ness in the church.

On the second Sunday we took the steam rack and pinion railway from Jenbach up to the beautiful lake Achensee. There we boarded a steamer. Matthew and Ruth played a game as we cruised along. It was a version of hide-and-seek thought up by Matthew. One of them would give a clue to an object on the ship and the other would then have to go and find it.

'Where is there a sock that's not on some-one's foot?' asked Matthew. Ruth couldn't work that one out but Christine—much to Matthew's chagrin—pointed to the wind-sock straight away.

We put into the village of Pertisau. In a souvenir shop Matthew took Ruth in tow and found two little mugs with 'Christine' on one and 'Robert' on the other.

'Mum, we want to buy these from Ruth and me for you and Dad—can we have our schillings?' he asked.

'That's a lovely idea, but are you sure? You haven't a lot of pocket money,' Christine replied.

'It's all right. Ruth will pay for one and I'll pay for the other,' Matthew assured her.

'But Ruth had a birthday before she came, she can afford it more than you.'

'Please Mum, we want to say thanks for such a great holiday.' And so Matthew presented us with our mugs.

'Where are you going to keep them?' he asked.

'We could put them in the lounge,' said Christine.

'I want mine in my study,' I said, feeling somehow that this was a significant present.

'And I could put mine in the kitchen with my collection of little vases,' responded Christine.

The next day we took the post-bus to the head of the valley at Hintertux to take the chair-lifts over a glacier to a mountain peak. I went with Ruth and told Matthew to go with his mother and look after her, as she had always been scared of chair-lifts.

'Is it as good as you expected, Matthew?' she asked as the first chair-lift started gaining height.

'Yes, Mum, it's great! See down there—you can see the first patches of snow.'

'I'd rather not look if you don't mind, please hold on to the rail, Matthew!'

'But I'm fine, Mum. I'm not scared.'

'No but I am—hold that rail!'

'Stop worrying, Mum.'

The chatter continued as we reached the end of the first stage. The next stage was a mini four-seater cable-car. Matthew noticed that Christine found this form of transport much more relaxing and was delighted that she could now enjoy the trip as fully as the rest of us. At the foot of the glacier we stopped at the hotel—captivated by the snow, the bright sun and the skiers—before taking the next two spectacular chair-lift rides to the summit. Matthew kept looking at his watch and wondering aloud what his school-friends—just back at school after half-term—would be doing. Being chair-lifted up a glacier in Austria was much more fun!

'Are you glad you came now, Mum?' he asked, as we started down from the summit.

'Oh yes, I'm used to it now. I wouldn't have missed this for anything, it's absolutely beautiful!' said Christine.

'It's the best thing I've ever done in my life,' responded Matthew. 'Have you noticed how quiet and peaceful it is?' Since Matthew had chatted non-stop all day, Christine's answer, amid family laughter, was, 'Well, it would be if you'd shut up.'

Ruth got cold on the way down in the chair-lift, and so I fumbled in the rucksack for a jersey. It happened to be Matthew's best grey one. Ruth put it on. Her brother, sitting behind, called out in tones of mock outrage, 'Hey that's mine! Take it off!' Ruth, unmoved and no stranger to hand-me-downs, replied with a giggle, 'It'll be mine one day, anyway!'

Once out of the chair-lift, the children found a playground which they turned into an 'assault course'. Then it was back on the bus and afterwards a round of crazy golf to finish a perfect day. In the hotel we read a Bible passage together, using Scripture Union's 'Time for the Family'. Then we prayed. Matthew's prayer was in a voice unusually full of feeling: 'Thank you God for the beautiful world you have given us to live in. Thank you for the mountains and the glacier and the snow. Thank you for the best and happiest day of my life.'

The following day, Tuesday, we went for a morning walk along the upper Ziller valley and then through alpine meadows to an alpine guest house called the *Steinerkogelhaus* which overlooked Mayrhofen. There we had a picnic lunch. Matthew peered down into the valley below to see the 12.13 steam train arrive at the station from Jenbach.

It was a hot day: the outside thermometer registered 100 Fahrenheit. We left the *Steinerkogelhaus* and began the walk down to the village—hoping for a dip in the outdoor swimming-pool there.

The path, through a coniferous forest, zig-zagged steeply. But it was broad and smooth—suitable for the average walker. We all had our hiking boots on and were very well equipped for the terrain.

About three-quarters of the way down, the children got a little ahead of Christine and me and were quickly out of sight on the next zigzag.

Suddenly I became aware that I could no longer hear their voices and so ran down to catch them up. We all knew the path, having been on it before, and were close to the village; so I ran on to the bottom, half-expecting the children to be waiting for me there—pleased at having arrived first.

There was no sign of them. I started running back up the path, shouting for them. Christine by now was somewhere behind me. In spite of a confusion of shouts from the swimming-bath and park just below, I thought I heard a cry for help and plunged off into the increasingly steep woodland to the side of the path. The cry came again—more clearly this time—followed by the faint voice of Ruth. Within a couple of minutes I came across Matthew.

He was lying against a tree with a terrible wound on his forehead. I thought, 'This isn't true: it's just a bad dream and I'll wake up in a minute.' At the same time I knew it wasn't a dream. I took out a bandage from the first aid kit in my rucksack and tied it round Matthew's head. I looked and felt for a pulse, a breath. There was no obvious sign of life.

But I was panting from the exertion of running up the hillside in the heat so it was hard to be sure. I gave him the kiss of life repeatedly.

After a while, I wrapped him in a silver foil emergency blanket which would have the effect of retaining body heat and propped him up against the tree in such a way that he would not fall if I had to leave him.

All this time I had been blowing the emergency whistle which I always carried in the rucksack—using what I thought was an international emergency code: seven pause seven.

Christine, meanwhile, had been returning up the path calling for the children and trying to interpret the confusing sounds echoing round the trees. Then she heard my whistle and knew something was seriously wrong.

She headed straight for the hotel to get the rescue services called out. Obviously they would be needed, but exactly why she had no idea.

As well as helping Matthew and blowing my whistle, I had also been trying to make contact with someone further up the wooded hillside who appeared to be with Ruth. I could shout to him, but the slope and the trees meant I couldn't see him. I discovered that he was a Welshman on holiday. He had been in the park when he had heard a scream from the hillside. Straight away he'd run up the slope in the direction of the voice. And, remarkably quickly, he had found Ruth. Out of all the people who must have heard the same scream, he was the only one who had responded. So now I knew that Ruth was lying injured but conscious somewhere further up the hill. After what seemed a long time during which, apparently, no one else was responding to my whistling, I decided to leave Matthew and make the perilous journey up to Ruth and our new Welsh friend.

She was lying still and there was a wound on her spine. But she was conscious and told me in a weak voice that she would be ok, so I only stayed a moment before leaving her to return to Matthew. The trip back was dangerous—very steep with small near-vertical rocky outcrops and much crumbling rock underfoot. I realised that if I were to climb straight down to Matthew I could dislodge the loose soil and stones and send them crashing down on him. So I made a detour, hoping not to get lost. I slithered and fell for some yards—collecting some cuts and bruises—before managing to grab and hold on to some tree roots. To my relief, I located Matthew again. But the sight of his still form filled me with dread afresh.

I started blowing my whistle again. More time passed. Then a policeman appeared, followed, a few minutes later, by a rescue team and a doctor. The doctor quickly confirmed my worst fears: Matthew was dead.

I cradled his head in my arms and howled and wept. My half-forgotten German had returned to me on holiday and I had begun to think in it as well as speak it.

'*Mein Sohn, Mein Sohn,*' I cried out over and over again. If Ruth had not been needing me, I don't know what I would have done in my anguish. But for her sake I had to keep going and stay sane. The team went up the hillside with the stretcher to collect Ruth while the policeman managed to persuade me to leave Matthew's body. It would have to be brought down later on. We made our way round the hillside to the path and arrived safely at the park.

I ran to Christine, put my arms around her and said, 'Oh my love, we have lost our Matthew.'

She had gathered from the rescue team's radio that Matthew had been injured. That anything worse had happened, had not occurred to her since the hillside hadn't seemed too steep or dangerous.

'No,' she said, unable for the moment to believe it.

'Yes, my darling, we have,' I replied.

I was covered in Matthew's blood. At a nearby trough I washed it off. Then we walked to the next field where a rescue helicopter was due to land. Several minutes later it arrived and then Ruth was brought across on her stretcher.

'How's Matthew?' was all she said.

'He's being brought down after you—you just worry about yourself,' I said, as we lifted her into the helicopter. It was only large enough for pilot, doctor and patient, so Ruth flew off to the *Klinik* in nearby Innsbruck without us. I had been a chaplain at a hospital with a spinal injuries unit and knew the risk of paralysis from spinal wounds. But I thought I had seen Ruth wiggle her toes and this gave me hope. I also remembered our feeling that, though we would not always have Matthew, we would always have Ruth. So I told myself she would be ok.

In the midst of her shock and grief and her struggle to come to terms with the news, Christine had an extraordinary sense of relief. She no longer needed to be afraid of what *might* happen: the worst *had* now happened. This didn't lessen her horror or anguish; relief was simply another emotion.

We were torn in two. Though anxious to go to Innsbruck to be with Ruth, we decided that

Christine must first see and feel Matthew's body. Some of the men involved in the rescue wanted to protect Christine from seeing Matthew, but we both realised that doing so would help her to accept the fact of his death. However distressing the experience, it is always better, I believe, that people should feel and see the body of their loved one.

I needed to touch Matthew again, too. On the hillside, wrapped in his emergency blanket in the heat of the day, he had still felt warm. I needed to be quite sure in my own mind that he was dead. He was to be brought to the chapel at the grave-yard just next door to the helicopter field. This news was enough to convince Christine that there was no possibility of mistake, but she still needed to see him.

Due to a mix up over keys, we had a long wait. Acceptance of sudden tragedy takes different people different lengths of time. I had had to accept our tragedy on the hillside—though I still wanted to touch Matthew for total confirmation of it. But the point of acceptance for Christine was during this wait—perhaps an hour or so after she had first heard the news. Such rapid acceptance was symptomatic of the speed with which God would move us on over the coming days.

As we waited in anguish, I leant my head against the outside wall of the beautiful chapel. On looking up, I realised that my head had been resting in the centre of a metal sculpture of Jesus' crown of thorns, as if to symbolise that I was now a man of sorrows and acquainted with grief. But it was comforting to realise that Jesus, supremely, had been such a man. Also, while waiting, we remembered more clearly our warning about Matthew and drew our first crumb of comfort together from it; and Christine, scared at the prospect of seeing Matthew's body, prayed for strength.

Her prayers were answered. Inside the chapel, looking at Matthew, her overwhelming feeling was that here was a battered, empty shell which our son had now discarded; he himself was not present with us—only his body was; the real Matthew had gone to be with his Saviour.

We were glad we were in a chapel—rather than a mortuary or hospital—as this could be for us a place of prayer as well as grief. The sight of Matthew, bloody but still beautiful, reminded me of his newborn body that bonfire night in the maternity block. Amidst the shock and anguish, I kept thinking of the verse about God loving the world so much that he gave his only Son to die for us on the cross (John 3:16).

I had just had my only son taken away from me but there was no circumstance that would ever have forced me to give him up, even for the whole world. Yet God had freely given his Son to die, and I wondered, awestruck, at his amazing love. And as I wondered, I felt his love and knew that I had been admitted to a strange and deep fellowship with him. I understood a little of what it costs truly to love, and realised something of the depth of divine suffering on the dark and hidden side of the love-gift of Jesus.

We were driven to Innsbruck that evening by Russell, one of our tour company representatives in Mayrhofen. We found the *Klinik* with a little difficulty and then located the ward where Ruth was to stay. We had already learnt by phone that she was having an operation, and we arrived on the ward just in time to see her wheeled in from the post-operation observation room. She was, of course, still asleep, but it was a help to see her and be reassured that we had not lost both our children.

Russell managed to book us into a small hotel very close to the *Klinik* and we spent a completely sleepless night there in howling anguish, tears and prayer. Why do people say that deep emotions are centred on the heart? Grieving comes from the guts. We felt physically sick for days—a feeling that would return with less intensity from time to time over the following months. Grief was felt in the abdomen, the throat, and the sides and back of the head—in fact, almost anywhere except the heart! It also seemed to get trapped inside a tortured forehead. I realised a little of what Jesus must have gone through in the Garden of Gethsemane just before his arrest, when, in his anguish, he sweated blood from his forehead. So I began to identify—albeit in my own limited human way—not only with God the Father but also with God the Son. He willingly drank his cup of suffering; mine had been forced upon me.

Our tears and anguish were a sign neither of weakness nor of lack of faith. We did not doubt God or feel any bitterness towards him. We were spared the great feelings of anger and bitterness that some of our Christian friends experienced for a while at the news. Rather, our tears were a natural and healthy reaction to a close and sudden bereavement.

We quickly decided to refuse any offers of sleeping pills or anti-depressants, and not to do any drinking. We felt that it was important to experience our grief naturally and sharply in order to get through its process healthily and quickly. The pent-up destructive power of suppressed grieving will unbalance the mind, damage the body or twist the soul. We should never fear the emotion-releasing power of an outward show of grief either in ourselves or others. It is cruel to collude in the suppression of people's grief because we find their grieving hard to cope with. It is kindness to help them face difficult situations head on. Big boys *do* cry, and must be allowed to.

We had no idea of the future that night— only of our loss and grief, and the horror our family had gone through that day. I would have died a hundred times over on that hillside rather than let this happen to Matthew, but there was nothing I could do to bring him back.

3
Ruth

At eight o'clock the following morning we made our way to Ruth's room at the *Klinik*.

'What sort of state will she be in?' we wondered.

We were very relieved to find her awake and coherent. She took the initiative, saying, as we came in through the door, 'How's Matthew?' I put my hand on her head and said, 'My darling, you must be very brave. We've lost him.' She blurted out, before she began to weep, 'Can we have another baby?'

Christine and I had already talked about this during the night at the hotel. Normal and sensible advice to the bereaved is not to make any major decisions for some time, but we had felt that God might want us to have a new baby. So I kissed Ruth and replied, 'I don't know, but we would like to try.'

'If we do, could we call him Matthew?' asked Ruth.

'No, my treasure,' I responded. 'We could

never replace Matthew. The baby would have to be somebody new with their own name.' I could understand her desire for another child to take the place of Matthew, but this would have been quite unfair to it. A child's interests, abilities, appearance, and character must be its own. To try to mould a child into Matthew's image would be cruel.

As we cried and talked that day, we gradually pieced together what had happened from Ruth's account. She explained, 'We were walking just ahead of you, holding hands and talking. We were planning what to do in the outdoor swimming-pool when we got down. And Matthew had been talking about heaven. He was always talking about heaven. Sometimes he'd even ask me about it and I'd say, "Matthew, how should I know what it's like? I should be asking you, not the other way round!" He was saying, "Isn't it wonderful in Austria with all these mountains and being on holiday! It's like being in heaven. Heaven must be wonderful as well. I can't make up my mind which is better—heaven or Austria. I don't know where I'd prefer to be."'

It seemed that Matthew and Ruth, deep in their conversation, instead of following the zigzag of the path, had carried on along a false path covered in pine needles just like the proper one. Suddenly Matthew had tripped over a tree root and fallen to his left where the ground had been particularly steep.

'I grabbed his hand again,' said Ruth, 'but he was too heavy for me. He said, "I'll fall but you'll be all right," and slipped out of my hand. He was thinking of me and didn't want me to fall after him. He started tumbling and rolling, and then he screamed, and then his head hit a tree and then he was quiet and I lost sight of him.'

Clearly Ruth had held on to Matthew for all she was worth, and his momentum had caused her to fall after him. She said, 'I went head over heels and closed my eyes and prayed that God would bring someone to rescue me. I hit my back and the top of my legs, and stopped. I gave one good scream and waited.'

Listening to Ruth was terribly distressing. Some of the story came out while I was away at the hospital office filling in forms, so Christine had to cope alone at times. But we had to find out what had happened, and Ruth had to be helped to tell the whole story rather than bottle it up inside. She also needed help with her feeling of guilt over the fact that she had not been able to hold on to Matthew firmly enough to stop him falling. I told her, 'Matthew was much heavier than you, my darling. You didn't have the weight and strength to drag him back. You were very brave to hold on to him so long that you were dragged down yourself. No one is going to blame you in any way.' But, however misplaced, guilt feelings are hard to defeat and we needed to say the same things to her again later on, when she heard about the accounts of the accident in the national papers, and started to worry that people reading them would blame her for not holding on strongly enough. In fact, the accounts made people realise how brave she had been.

Later that morning I had to go back to the

hotel to phone our families and friends with the news. First of all, I phoned my sister and brother-in-law, Sue and Keith, who lived close to us in Sheffield, with the request that they would go and tell my parents in person. To them and to the others whom I phoned later I added, 'I want you to know that we have always known that one day we would lose Matthew—God warned us before he was born and he will take care of us now.' I couldn't remember Christine's brother's phone number or address and so had to phone her parents direct. I then made a list of as many phone numbers of Christian friends round the country as I could remember and phoned Tim and Helen Gregory to ask them to circulate the news to them. Tim was our reader at St Mark's, bearing the burden of leadership for the church while I was away, and theirs was the only local phone number I could recall in my state of shock and grief. The story had been in the Austrian press that morning and so would be in the English press the next day, and I didn't want friends and relatives to learn what had happened from the papers; also we needed to mobilise people to pray for us. But having to phone up family and close friends with the news was almost as bad as telling Christine and Ruth had been. As I put the phone down for the last time and realised the enormity of the impact of my message on other people's lives, I cried out to God, 'How many more terrible things do I have to do today?'

We went through our sharpest, deepest grief that day, and our minds were all filled with images of the hillside and of Matthew's fall and suffering. I had been with Matthew for a very long

time trying to revive him and I was reliving that
nightmare. Christine remembered hearing a loud
scream from the woods and concluded from Ruth's
account that this had probably been Matthew.
Together with the images of confusion, shouting
and helplessness, in her imagination she kept
seeing him scream and fall time and again. Ruth
was supposed to spend the day dozing following
her injuries and operation, but each time she
closed her eyes she had a vivid mental picture of
the accident.

'I can't sleep, I can only see Matthew falling,'
she said to us.

'Let's pray that Jesus will take that away,' I
said, and, for the first of many times, prayed, 'Dear
Lord Jesus, thank you that you love Ruth and care
for her. Please help her to stop seeing Matthew's
fall when she closes her eyes and please help her to
sleep soundly and without any nasty dreams.'

The absolute worst time for our grief
seemed to be over by about teatime when strength
and comfort began to flow into us. I could feel
courage and resolution flowing into me; it was like
a physical sensation. Having had similar, though
not so dramatic, experiences in the past, I had no
doubt as to the cause: Tim and Helen had done
their job and Christians in England had begun to
pray for us. So Christine was able to grasp that
Matthew had only fallen once; that it had all been
over in a couple of seconds; and that the endless
suffering which the replays in our minds had been
suggesting was not in keeping with the facts.

Another turning point for Christine came
while she was hearing from Ruth more details

about the accident. At one point, feeling desperate, she went out into the corridor to be by herself, while I stayed with Ruth. There she reached her lowest point, wanting God's help but way beyond coherent thought and prayer. She was in the depths of a grief deeper than she had realised anyone could ever reach. It was then that a verse was projected into her mind with great clarity; one she had always previously thought applicable to the dead and dying, rather than to the bereaved:

'Even though I walk through the valley of the shadow of death,
I will fear no evil, for you are with me;
your rod and your staff they comfort me' (Psalm 23:4).

Suddenly Christine realised that she, in her bereavement, was the one who was in death's dark shadow and that therefore the promise was for her: God was right down there with her. The same was true for the rest of the family. We had been in the valley of the shadow of death physically and literally, and we were still there emotionally. But we were not alone: God was with us to comfort us. As for Matthew, he had passed very quickly through that valley into the heaven where he had always half-wanted to be anyway.

But could she be sure of that? Her desperate need was for reassurance that Matthew had indeed gone to be with the Lord in heaven. We had a pocket-sized New Testament from which Christine sought solace. Two verses, in particular, seemed to leap out of the page at her. The first was:

Whoever acknowledges me before men, I will also
acknowledge him before my Father in heaven
(Matthew 10:32).

Christine's mind went back to the football
ground and Mission England the previous
summer. There and then Matthew had acknowledged Jesus, so she could trust Jesus to return the
compliment.

The other verse came in a chapter which the
four of us had studied together in Mayrhofen
about how God's people had trusted him in the
past and pleased him by their faith. It was:

By faith we understand that the universe was
formed at God's command, so that what is seen was
not made out of what was visible (Hebrews 11:3).

Christine remembered how Matthew, on the
night before he'd died, had prayed—thanking
God, after our day on the glacier, for the beautiful
world he had made; and felt reassured that he was
in the company of those who had died in a state of
faith and trust in God. Surely after the best day of
his life on earth, even as he had talked about how
wonderful heaven must be, Matthew had gone to
be with his heavenly Father.

But if God was ministering to us through
verses of Scripture, he was ministering to Ruth
more directly. That evening, we prayed again for
the gift of sleep for her, and she eventually
dropped off into a fitful slumber, her face still
registering the same mix of mental anguish and
physical pain. There were scratches, cuts and
bruises from her head to her ankles. Only her feet
had escaped, protected by her strong walking

boots. She had a wound and severe bruising round the perineum, which had been repaired with stitches. The wound on the lower spine had required ligaments to be sewn back together.

But when she awoke about an hour later her face had miraculously changed and cleared. She looked serene and was smiling.

'God and Matthew have spoken to me,' she said to Christine who was with her. 'It wasn't a dream, it was much more than that. They were real and they were outside me. God held my hand tight, I could really feel it. Matthew said to me, "You are safe and I am safe, so why worry?"'

'And what did God say to you, my love?' Christine asked.

'He said, "I love Matthew even more than you do, and I want him with me now."'

Ruth believed the voices and trusted God; she felt greatly strengthened and reassured. For the first time in her life, and at her time of greatest need, God had spoken directly to her. She could trust him to take care of Matthew. Ruth was to know many ups and downs in her adjustment to bereavement, but that encounter was her turning point.

Christine and I managed about four hours of sleep that night, and then forced down a bread roll for breakfast. Our throats were too constricted to feel any desire to eat, but we knew that we needed to begin to nurse ourselves back to some sort of strength and normality. I then had to leave Christine with Ruth while I took a taxi back to Mayrhofen to conduct some business with the undertaker and to collect our things from the hotel. Everyone was very upset and kind, especially the staff and guests at our hotel. For the first—but by no means the last—time I found myself trying to comfort others about Matthew, telling them, in a mixture of dodgy German and pigeon English, that we were Christians and believed Matthew was with God in heaven.

I found I could cope with the expected things—even with something like packing Matthew's clothes and teddy bear into suitcases. It was the unexpected ones that caused me to break down and weep. We all experienced this a number of times in the following weeks. It happened first on the drive back to Innsbruck with Russell, our tour company representative. The road in the Ziller valley followed the narrow gauge railway which Matthew had so loved. His special favourite, and mine, had been the twice-a-day steam train. As we rounded a bend in the car, there it was coming towards us, working hard to climb the valley. It was overwhelming to think that Matthew had been so full of life and fun on that same train just a few days before.

Meanwhile, Ruth had been summoned to the neurology department for a computer tomography. The neurologist, Dr Mayr, was most kind and spoke perfect English. Christine ended up in the computer room with him, watching the pictures of Ruth's insides coming up on the screen. The computer programme was in English so she was able to follow what was happening. The results were excellent with no serious damage to the spine being visible.

Christine was still seeking reassurances of

Matthew's place in heaven and longed for God to speak to her directly as he had to Ruth. But, meanwhile, she had her New Testament and there (in 1 Corinthians 15:42 ff.) she read of the contrast between the resurrection body and the earthly body. Matthew's injuries had been ugly, but the promise was that his resurrection body would be perfect and beautiful.

That afternoon reinforcements arrived. My sister Sue and her husband Keith had planned to drive out to be with us. But their car had needed attention; also they'd realised that they were both too tired and upset to risk a long drive so it had been decided that Sue should fly out alone. She had never flown before and the prospect terrified her: the thought of planes made her feel claustrophobic. But she had taken her courage in both hands and set off for Manchester airport. There she had bullied the man at the ticket desk into selling her a ticket despite the fact that she had no cheque card—having left this at home. True courage, as we had been realising ourselves, consists of going through with things that terrify you. She had done that—and it was a thrill for all three of us to see her come through the door into Ruth's hospital room.

We left Sue alone with Ruth for a couple of hours as we took our first break. Ruth spent the whole time telling Sue about the accident and how Matthew was safe with God, for she was still glowing from the encounter in her sleep the evening before. As we returned Sue said, 'That £300 plane ticket's worth it already. What a privilege to talk to Ruth, or rather to listen to her!'

Christine, too, had been wonderfully brave and composed while grieving most deeply. We were taking turns to console each other and keep each other going. I felt very proud of my brave family.

During this time we had very strong mental images of Matthew. Always resenting the very few hours a night he spent sleeping, he used to wake up first and get in a couple hours of play before the rest of us stirred. Christine now saw or imagined him enjoying himself in heaven and saying, 'It's great over here, Mum: I don't need to sleep at all now.' I kept seeing him leaning nonchalantly against heaven's door and saying, with his cheeky grin, as I approached it, 'Oh hello! What took you so long?' Ruth believed she had heard his voice in her encounter with God. Christine's father cried over Matthew each morning for several days until he heard what seemed to be his voice simply saying, 'Don't cry, Poppa.'

What are we to make of these things? Perhaps Matthew was allowed to help us in our time of need.

Sue had brought with her a long list of signatures from a special memorial service held for Matthew at St Mark's the previous evening—the day after Matthew's death. St Mark's was a fairly ordinary middle-sized parish church serving an old village which had also become a suburb of Sheffield. We had only been there for two years but, after Tim and Helen had phoned round with the news and a request to get together that evening, there had been a great outpouring of grief and of love for us and the building had been packed for the service. The congregation had included most of Matthew's friends and the teachers from the village junior school. It was an immense help to know that the church and village were pulling together, praying for us and supporting us. Other friends in other churches also began to meet together to pray for us. Phone calls were beginning to get through to the hotel and the ward office in the *Klinik*. I took about ten phone calls that day from various parts of England; from these we began to get an inkling of a vast network of prayer all over the country.

We coveted every one of those prayers because we experienced their uplifting effect on us as we began to know 'the peace of God which passes all understanding' alongside our grief and anguish. About three times in the following week while praying with Christine, I had a strong physical sensation of strength and courage flowing into me in the area of my back and shoulders. I believe that was God answering our friends' prayers and our own. Every morning as I woke up, my first thought was a prayer for courage to meet the coming day. Courage was what I chiefly needed both for myself and in order to be a strength to Christine and Ruth. Prayer became a lifeline to God far more precious and powerful than in normal circumstances.

Joseph Scriven lost his fiancée in a drowning accident only days before their wedding, and, immediately after her funeral, he wrote:

> *What a friend we have in Jesus,*
> *All our sins and griefs to bear!*
> *What a privilege to carry*
> *Everything to God in prayer!*

O what peace we often forfeit,
O what needless pain we bear—
All because we do not carry
Everything to God in prayer.

We were grateful that we had been praying people *before* Matthew's death so that the channel to God was already open and in place for us. Without prayer we might not even have survived; with it we could triumph!

The next day, Friday, the English community in Innsbruck began to rally round. One lady began to visit Ruth in hospital and bring her chocolates and books. She was visibly shaken and moved by Ruth's courage and testimony of faith. Another took our clothes, and washed them most beautifully for us. Jonathan, an English student at the Roman Catholic Seminary in Innsbruck, brought us all the equipment needed to make tea and coffee in the hotel room—and a whole Bible, including, of course, the Old Testament.

Several times during the week Christine had found she needed to pray for courage to take on something difficult. Now she felt it was time for her to talk to her parents on the phone and reassure them that she was all right in herself. As I handed the phone to her, she felt all the strength and confidence which she needed in order to minister to them, flowing into her.

We were also getting to know Ruth's doctors and nurses. Her surgeon, Dr Hager, was a lion of a man with a booming voice which woke every baby on the corridor at ward-round time. He exuded confidence and reassurance and gave us every kindness and consideration. He was clearly loved by the nurses, who were all specially trained *kinderschwestern*—children's nurses. Generally speaking, the doctors' English was good, whereas that of the nurses was much more limited, so I was often required to act as interpreter for Ruth—spending quite a lot of my time either translating her requests to the nurses or their requests back to her. This at least made me feel useful.

For Ruth, the worst times were going to sleep in the evening, waking up alone at night, and the first few minutes of waking and remembering each morning. Sue, Christine and I developed a rota for sitting with Ruth as she went to sleep at night, calling back at 10.30 p.m. to check on her, and being in her room as she woke at around 6.45 a.m. The hospital staff allowed us to break their visiting rules in this way, as they were very aware of the fact that they were treating a patient in shock and grief as well as one with physical injuries. They co-operated with us in ministering healing, in its widest sense, to Ruth.

It was becoming apparent that Ruth was mending quite fast. Her face was becoming visible again as the scratches, cuts and bruises began to heal. It was a daily miracle each morning to see her waking—her face looking more clear and beautiful each time. The scratches and bumps were not just receding; they were disappearing altogether! Our main worry was neurological, in view of Ruth's spinal injury. But we always felt that she would make a full recovery. Just as our premonition about Matthew had come true, so too, we believed, would our certainty about having an unimpaired

Ruth always with us.

At first the doctors said she would be in hospital for three weeks. This was shortened to two, and by the weekend they were talking about ten days. This was no surprise to us because we knew that hundreds of Christians were praying for her rapid and complete recovery, and we were trusting God to answer those prayers. We also knew how important it was for all three of us to get home together in good time and order for Matthew's funeral. The thought of Ruth being kept in Austria while the funeral took place in England was untenable. I believe there is nothing worse for a child than to be excluded from a family funeral. Children have the same psychological needs as adults and can suffer and be damaged emotionally if they are shut out.

Thanks to our new Bible from Jonathan, Friday was also the day the Old Testament began to speak to us:

> Because of the Lord's great love we are not consumed, for his compassions never fail.
> They are new every morning; great is your faithfulness . . .
> For men are not cast off by the Lord for ever.
> Though he brings grief, he will show compassion, so great is his unfailing love.
> For he does not willingly bring affliction or grief to the children of men (Lamentations 3:22, 23, 31–33).

We started to use these verses each morning, and to pray at the start of each day for God's compassion and faithfulness. There was no way we could yet face the future as a whole, so we had to pray for grace just to take us through the day in front of us.

With the better news about how long Ruth would be in hospital, I felt more able to think about the funeral service. Irrationally, or so it had seemed to the family who had teased me about it, I had packed my service book with the holiday gear. It contained the funeral service. All arrangements would have to be made from Innsbruck since we would need to have the service as soon as we returned to England. Another 'coincidence' had been Sue's insistence, when she and Keith had had to renew their family passport not long before our holiday, on having her name first so she could travel independently should the need arise—which it did; a third was the fact that Christine had brought on holiday with us her favourite photograph of our golden retriever, Sam. We'd teased her about that, but now the picture came into its own, taking pride of place by Ruth's bedside. Sam had always been especially Ruth's dog, and the knowledge that he would be waiting for her when she got home was a great boost to her morale. In these and other details we began to realise that God had been planning in advance to sustain us through what he had known would happen.

I had been due to preach on the Sunday after the holiday on:

> I want to know Christ and the power of his resurrection and the fellowship of sharing in his sufferings, becoming like him in his death (Philippians 3:10).

'The fellowship of sharing in his sufferings' was the strange and terrible fellowship to which I had felt myself admitted. Now I was beginning to share in the power of Christ's resurrection, as my resurrection faith was being strengthened by answered prayer and all the tokens of God's presence and planning. Christian friends began to write to us, quoting this verse as being for us; and I realised that just as Good Friday had to come before Easter Sunday, so our suffering was the prelude and precondition to really knowing the power of his resurrection.

But the spiritual struggle had to take place in the context of all kinds of urgent practical problems. I had been trying to arrange for Matthew's body to be flown back with us. But I was told that this would be impossible, as a *post mortem* would have to be carried out in England. So, reluctantly, late on Friday afternoon, I agreed to let Matthew be flown to London and then taken to Sheffield. The sense of loss and separation that this occasioned was eased somewhat by remembering that we were only dealing with his earthly remains. Matthew himself was in his spiritual body in heaven. Even so the wrench was still real and painful.

Christine had taken the brunt of being with Ruth in the *Klinik*, and so, on the Saturday morning, Sue and I sent her out to do some shopping. As she wandered around some of the places we had visited as a family a few days previously, she had the chance to confront again the questions that kept recurring: Was God really in control? Was Matthew really in heaven?

She went again into the cathedral—a building which Matthew had greatly enjoyed, trying out all the confessional boxes and mesmerized by the ornate ceiling and fittings. But the cathedral was not the right place for Christine's comfort that day. However, outside, a local band was playing *Plaisirs D'Amour*. I had recently written some Christian words to this song for her music group to sing in church. Now she remembered one of the verses:

> *He cried for me, in grief at Gethsemane,*
> *By my sin nailed to a tree Jesus died for me.*
> *He rose for me, in triumph setting me free,*
> *From death to eternity, Jesus rose for me.*

Battling with pain, grief, guilt and confusion, and with the question 'why?'—Christine went back to our hotel room and opened her Bible. Some words hit her like a bolt of lightning:

'Come now, let us reason together,' says the Lord.
'Though your sins are like scarlet, they shall be as white as snow;
though they are red as crimson, they shall be like wool' (Isaiah 1:18).

On one level God seemed to be saying, through that verse, that even if Christine had sinned by letting Matthew out of her sight on the walk, or by doing something even more terrible than that, he would make it right again. At another, through the first part of the verse—'Come now, let us reason together'—he seemed to be telling her (so clearly that the words were almost audible): 'Come on woman, pull yourself together; don't do it on your own; reason it out with me; we can sort this out if we get together on it. Lift your-self above your feelings and be logical. Write down everything that's happening so you can see clearly all that I am doing.'

And so Christine knew that she must write things down so that God's activity and reasoning could become clear to us. The notes she made that morning, and the diary she kept thereafter, form the basis of this book and were a means of helping us to piece the whole story together and reason it all out with the Lord.

A phone call at lunchtime informed us that the story had been on television and in the national press at home the previous day, and that the children's picture had been in all the papers. Christine's reaction was to say that it was a privilege to be trusted by God with such an experience in the public eye. He was giving us the unwanted oppor-tunity to handle Matthew's death and its aftermath as Christians under the public gaze. Our responsi-bility was to honour the name of Christ and to testify to the powerful resurrection faith he was cultivating in us. I was beginning to have plenty of chances to do this by talking, in my half-forgotten but fast-returning German, with hospital and hotel staff, visitors from Mayrhofen, the other children on the ward and their parents. The children would ask Ruth if she had any brothers or sisters, and I would step in to explain what had happened and what our faith was about.

It was a special thrill over the next few days to discover some fellow Christians. One was the lady at the hotel reception. She took all our tele-phone calls while we were at the *Klinik* and did her best to relay them accurately. It amused us when she spoke of Sue, who was Mrs Pennington, as 'Mrs Paddington'! She expressed her sympathy in a mixture of English and German.

One day she told us: 'A year ago my fiancé was killed in an accident just before our wedding day. Friends gave me a Bible with some verses marked and it has been the most important thing for me. I don't know how I could have survived without my Bible and my friends. I am going next week to spend my week's holiday with them.' Then she took out from under the counter a well-worn Bible—proof of her dependence on its strength and support. Our hearts went out to her, as hers did to us.

The great event of Saturday was the removal of Ruth's drain tube, which had been causing her a great amount of pain and discomfort because of the severe bruising between her legs. When the tube had been removed, we helped Ruth to take her first few, slow, difficult and painful steps to the toilet at the other side of her room. Though very stiff and needing support, she proved that she could walk again! So we began to firm up plans with the doctors to go home together in the middle of the following week.

4
Aftermath

It had rained most of the time since our arrival in Innsbruck, as though the heavens were joining in our tears. But Sunday dawned clear and beautiful and full of bird-song. Here was a new week and a new beginning. The mountains are amazingly close to Innsbruck and stupendously high. The four of us had shared a great love of mountains as places of beauty and refreshment, both physical and spiritual. Now their sheer and rocky slopes were all around me; painful and poignant, their dangerous beauty beckoned. Feelings of guilt at having led Matthew to a dangerous place, albeit near the bottom of a small hill close to a public park, rose within me. How could I ever go walking in hills again? How could anyone be trusted in my care again? All my hobbies and interests had been developed and shared with Matthew—railways, model railways, football and mountains. How could I ever have the heart to take up these things again? I could take some comfort from the relationship we had enjoyed. Yet I knew I had lost my best friend as well as my son, and the hole in my life was all the greater.

All this came to me as I walked in the clear morning air to Ruth's room at the *Klinik*. We had felt in need of receiving communion and had contemplated going to an English service in Innsbruck that Jonathan had told us about. But in the end we had decided to hold our own service in Ruth's room, so that we could include Ruth. One reason for needing the service was our inner battle with guilt feelings and our desire to say the confession and hear the words of forgiveness in the absolution. Guilt feelings, we knew, were important to deal with because of their destructive potential. It was during Sunday that we began to work through ours.

We became aware of three types of guilt inside us. The first and most important was the guilt arising from feeling responsible for what had happened. When someone, particularly a child, dies, we find it hard to accept. We can't just shrug our shoulders and say, 'It's just one of those things.' In Western society we desperately try to believe in our supposed 'right' to live to a good old age. A child's death is a terrible and threatening challenge to that belief. Something or somebody must be to blame for it. Sometimes the blame is fastened (rightly or wrongly) on a third party, such as the doctor or the driver of the other car. More often, loved ones blame themselves—'This person depended on me and now they are dead. I must have let them down.'

Such guilt feelings may or may not be based on reality. The doctor may have been negligent or the driver of the other car drunk. In our own case, we had been on a family walk when the tragedy had occurred. The children had been in our care when they'd wandered out of our sight and been killed or injured. As caring and responsible parents, we felt guilty and wondered how we could ever live with ourselves again.

We found it a great help to try to look at the situation objectively. We had not been on an obviously difficult mountain track, but on a path up which pensioners sometimes shuffled in sandals. Our travel insurance company when contacted had tried to evade responsibility by claiming that we'd been on a dangerous path, but the police had given them a report saying that we had in no way been foolhardy or negligent; so they then had to accept their responsibility. We were very grateful for that report for our own peace of mind and because it helped us financially. Also, we knew that the children had been wearing good walking boots, that they were careful and sensible walkers and that they had been on the same path a few days earlier. They had simply missed their way for a few yards, and during those few moments Matthew had tripped over a tree root and fallen. It had been a freak accident.

Nevertheless, the children *had* been in our care and we *had* let them get out of sight: it was for this reason that I felt in most need of forgiveness. It was a help to remember that Mary and Joseph had lost Jesus for four days when he'd been twelve years old. It helped too when people said to us, as several parents did, 'What ten-year-old doesn't slip out of sight on a family walk?' or, 'You can't hold the hand of a ten-year-old all the time.'

I also had the problem of wondering whether there was anything I could have done to save Matthew's life after I had found him. He had been in the St John Ambulance and had probably known at least as much as I about resuscitation and life-saving. I feared what the *post mortem* might say, while continuing to believe that he'd died instantly after receiving the wound on his forehead.

Distressingly, some of the press reports suggested that we had been taking a short cut. This was not true, but we worried that family and friends might privately think the accident was our fault, even though they would never be cruel enough to suggest this. So we decided to tell them all, as accurately as possible, exactly what had happened.

Much more important than what others felt or thought, was the way *we* saw it ourselves and the way *God* saw it. Christine had realised, in the hotel room the previous day, that even if she had deliberately killed someone, God could still forgive her. When Jesus was dying on the cross, he said of those who had crucified him, 'Father, forgive them, for they do not know what they are doing' (Luke 23:34). Though we were trying to be objective, we were too involved to be clear as to how much forgiveness we needed. We hoped that it wasn't *too* much; but however great or small our real guilt was, we wanted to confess it:

Almighty God our Heavenly Father, we have sinned against you and against our fellow men, in thought and word and deed, through negligence,

through weakness, through our own deliberate
fault . . .

It was the 'negligence' that was uppermost in
my mind. I prayed, 'If I have been negligent, Lord,
I am truly sorry.' As I pronounced the absolution
in Ruth's hospital room, I knew that we were forgiven for anything that needed forgiving, and that
we were restored and cleansed by a compassionate
God.

When the guilt feelings came again in the
months to come, they would be dealt with in the
same way—by confession and forgiveness. They
were too strong, of course, to be dealt with all at
once, just as severe illness is usually too strong to be
dealt with by the first dose of medicine. Similarly,
many other emotions which we worked through in
Innsbruck, needed to be worked through again in
subsequent months in a deeper and longer-lasting
way. God's grace was not cheap, instant, happy-
clappy magic, but profound, and therefore its out-
working needed time.

Even more insidious than the guilt of feeling
responsible was the guilt from regrets. We wept
over times when—had we not been too busy or
tired—we might have taken more interest in
Matthew's world or been more patient and
generous with him. He had asked for an ice-cream
just before leaving the *Steinerkogelhaus* and
Christine had said, 'No,'—intending to buy him
one at the bottom but not saying so. Now she
regretted having sounded harsh.

Perhaps we had less to feel guilty about than
some parents but we knew we were less than

perfect and now there was no chance to put anything right. Since we never know when we will be parted from those close to us, how important it is to have nothing between us, nothing left unsaid, no situation left unresolved! Tomorrow may be too late to sort things out.

The same applies to our relationship with God. We never know how long we've got to sort things out with him in this life. We were more than relieved by the knowledge that Matthew had been nurtured into a Christian faith of his own before his death, because the biggest regret of all would have been if he had died in a state of rejection of Christ and our faith.

The realisation, thrust upon us with such great force, that tomorrow may be too late, caused us to reassess our priorities in life, with a view to minimising the chances of having to face this guilt from regrets.

On the plane coming home, Christine saw many important-looking businessmen and reflected that, as far as she was concerned, the dog-eared list of signatures from the memorial service at St Mark's was far more important than all the papers and documents in their impressive-looking brief-cases. The newspapers were full of trivia, apart from events in South Africa—where the never-ending cycle of murderous funerals seemed even more terrible than ever. Priorities, we felt, must be people not profit; relationships not materialism; time with the children not housework; making the most of people while we have them and leaving nothing unsaid or undone. In particular, I resolved to explain the Christian gospel in my day-to-day ministry more clearly. Time might be short and I didn't want to be responsible for any of my parishioners dying without having heard from my lips and behaviour the news of eternal life with which God had entrusted me.

In the *Klinik* that Sunday, we did more than resolve to live differently in the future. First, we confessed our imperfections as parents, and accepted that God had 'forgotten' the things we had regrets over, even if we hadn't. Secondly, we began the painful but healing process of reminiscing about the good times and memories, of which there were many.

But it was Ruth who showed us the way to the third and most helpful thing that we did.

'I've thought of a way of talking to Matthew,' she confided in me.

'Oh, yes,' I responded dubiously. 'What do you do?'

'I just talk to God and he passes the message on,' she said triumphantly.

That set my mind in a whirl. Should I encourage her or not? Among most Christians there is a taboo on praying for the dead on the grounds that our destiny is determined by our response to God on this earth. Christians rightly steer clear of spiritualism and of all situations such as raising the late lamented Uncle Herbert to have a chat from the beyond with Aunty Nell. At the same time, we believed that Matthew would be with God in heaven and that God hears and responds to our prayers. So why would God refuse to pass a message on?

In the Apostles' Creed each Sunday,

Christians say that they believe in, among other things, 'the communion of saints'—the fellowship of all God's people, living and departed. It occurred to me that we miss so much when we forget that we are in fellowship with Christians who have gone before.

So after a few seconds' hesitation and groping, as some of those thoughts flashed through my mind, I responded, 'You're right Ruth; we're not cut off from Matthew because we're not cut off from God. Well done! Thank you!' Then Christine and I also prayed to God, thanking him that Matthew was now safe with him, and asking him to pass on the message that we loved Matthew and always wanted the best for him, and that all was well between us. We felt we could do this while still continuing to be orthodox Christian believers and it helped enormously in coping with our guilt from regrets. Our relationship with Matthew would never come to an end. Though parted irretrievably, we were bound together invisibly in that eternal fellowship of all those, living and departed, who love God and surround his throne.

The final guilt we faced that day and subsequently, was the guilt we felt about enjoying anything. For our communion service, I already had some blackcurrant juice from the hospital snack bar to use as wine, but I had to ask one of the nurses for some bread. She brought this, beautifully laid out on a tray with paper napkins. Then I tried to work out the German to explain that the four of us would be having a communion service and to ask the nurses to leave us alone for half an hour or so. I couldn't remember the word for 'communion' and so looked it up in the dictionary. There were two alternatives. I chose the first one and was just about to use it when something stopped me. Hastily, I checked its English translation in the other half of the dictionary and discovered that I had been a hair's breadth from asking the nurses to leave us alone so we could have sexual intercourse! We laughed together about this, visualising how the nurses would have responded, but then felt guilty at enjoying something, even momentarily, so soon after Matthew's death.

Ever since the time when Queen Victoria mourned endlessly for Albert, decent people have been expected to be inconsolable, especially after the death of a child. We, like Victoria, should not have been amused. At least our feelings of guilt told us so, both then and later—whenever some colour or enjoyment returned to our lives. Were we heartless, uncaring parents to find pleasure in living? Or did we have some deep psychological problem of lack of acceptance resulting in a fragile 'let's pretend' exterior?

Time and again in the weeks that followed we found ourselves feeling guilty at apparently coping so well with what had happened. Friends would be surprised at how strong and 'normal' we seemed and would warn us that we were 'too good to last'. It was a classic case of Christians not believing the answers to their own prayers, for we were in truth upheld for a long time on a great barrage of prayer rising from Christians all over the country.

So how were we to cope with the 'guilt' of coping and finding pleasure in life again? As

Christine and I talked this through we realised that to shrink from life's good things is to shrink from God himself, for he is the source of all true pleasure, joy in living and peace of mind. Also, we had a responsibility to Ruth, to each other, to our friends, family and church, to build a happy and secure home again. Equally, we owed it to God to grow into that wholeness of mind and spirit that he desires for us all.

After all, we were not mourning without hope as others did. We believed Matthew to be in heaven, where we would one day join him. In his dying and rising, Jesus had drawn the sting of death and opened the gate of glory. Jesus had defeated the horrible accident that had happened to Matthew and had turned it into his highway to heaven. Why should Christine and I turn ourselves into useless, inconsolable wrecks as though we were people without hope and without the peace of God which passes all understanding? God's desire for us was to make us whole and at peace with him, within ourselves, and with our fellow man. Our job was to co-operate with him in his task of rebuilding us in the weeks and years ahead; and if the Master-builder was getting on with the job ahead of human schedules, who were we to complain?

And so we realised—most clearly in the *Klinik*, later at Matthew's funeral, and then from time to time in the subsequent months—that Christians could experience simultaneously two different kinds of emotions. On the one hand there were grief, emptiness, longing and pain; on the other, peace, joy, hope, and assurance both of the love of God and of an eternal future. There was no shallow self-deception here: two deeply-felt sets of emotions were experienced together—one drawing the sting of the other not by repressing it but by mingling with it and transforming it.

How we could have coped with true or false guilt in these three different areas, if we had not been Christians—I have no idea. At the same time, emotions are untidy and persistent and it would be foolish triumphalism to claim that we had them all sorted out quickly and neatly. But as Christians we had the tools for the job. In that communion service in Ruth's room there were the confession and absolution to cleanse us from the guilt from feeling responsible; and there was prayer to cope with the guilt from regrets. We talked with the God who had Matthew at his side; and we had the spiritual food of the body and blood of Christ—medicine from the one who had drawn death's sting—to restore to us our capacity for living life in all its fulness. We could truly say: Thanks be to God for the victory of faith, which knows that there is nothing in all creation—no guilt, real or imagined, no agony of mind—that can separate us from the love of God in Christ Jesus our Lord!

At the communion service, I was at a loss for a Bible reading!

'Has anyone got any suggestions?' I asked as we got under way. Ruth took charge at once.

'Can we have Psalm 91?' she asked. 'It was Matthew's favourite psalm, and it's mine. I think he knew it practically off by heart. I'd like to have it at the funeral.' Matthew and Ruth had learned this psalm just over a year earlier at a children's week at church led by John Hattam from Scripture Union.

'All right, you can read it yourself, Ruth, but I'm afraid we've only got Jonathan's *Revised Standard Version*, which has got old-fashioned language in it. Can you manage?' I asked.

'Oh yes, I think so,' she said, propping herself a little higher on the pillows. And so the most special part of a very special service was to hear Ruth, just eight years old, painfully injured and freshly grieving, faultlessly read her psalm in its old-fashioned language. The words spoke deeply to and about us all. The psalm began:

> He who dwells in the shelter of the Most High, who abides in the shadow of the Almighty,
> will say to the Lord, 'My refuge and my fortress; my God in whom I trust' (Psalm 91:1,2 RSV).

That, we felt, was about Matthew—where he dwelt, how he trusted, and where he was abiding now.

The accident had happened in the heat of the day so it was not unnatural for us to have a sense of dread at midday or whenever the weather was sunny and hot. Ruth, however, had her greatest fears at night. As she closed her eyes, the horror would return. But the psalm said:

> You will not fear the terror of the night, nor the arrow that flies by day,
> nor the pestilence that stalks in darkness, nor the destruction that wastes at noonday (Psalm 91:5, 6 RSV).

There was strength for us all in the reassurance that we had nothing to fear—even at our 'fearful' times: noonday and night. Life would certainly have its difficulties but if God could handle a tragedy as great as Matthew's death, he could handle anything that might come our way.

Because he cleaves to me in love, I will deliver him;
I will protect him, because he knows my name.
When he calls to me I will answer him;
I will be with him in trouble, I will rescue him and honour him.
With long life I will satisfy him, and show him my salvation (Psalm 91:14–16 RSV).

These verses were for all three of us, promising God's protection and presence with us in trouble—something we were already experiencing. They also promised, we believed, that God would honour our trust in him and that our future lives together would be long.

Only a child reading a psalm—yet through that God spoke his words to his children in need: words which we believed had a personal application to us. Surely his goodness and mercy would follow us all the days of our lives and we would dwell with Matthew in the House of the Lord for ever!

By the end of the weekend we had sketched out an outline for Matthew's funeral service and on Monday we received a letter from the Bishop of Doncaster, Bill Persson. He had known Matthew quite well, and I had already asked him by phone to take the service for us. His letter gave episcopal authority to the view that there would be trains in heaven and he suggested that Matthew would now be happily engaged getting them to run to time! We also received a delightful letter from Greg

Holyand—a colleague due to preach for me at St Mark's whom I had met only once briefly in the past, and Christine not at all. Christian love and fellowship is such that we felt the prayer and support of those who did not really know us, just as much as the prayer and support of our closest friends. Also my sister Sue and Christine, who had always got on well, were now even closer—like sisters. Christine felt that this was one of the first gains to come out of her loss.

My own days continued to be plagued by telephonic battles with our travel insurance company. The company did all it could to evade or reduce its obligations to us. After the police report had left them no alternative but to accept liability, they tried to move us from our hotel to another one much further away from the *Klinik* because it was £1.50 per night cheaper. I said I would pay the difference and stay put. They then tried to say that one of us should return home on the Saturday on our charter flight from Munich, for which we had, of course, already paid. Such pressure we found almost unbelievably heartless. Our tour operators and the doctors were very helpful in trying to make the company behave more reasonably, but they were still making life difficult. They had promised to phone the *Klinik* on Monday about a discharge date for Ruth so that they could make travel arrangements for us. But they failed to keep their promise so, in the afternoon, I returned to the hotel to phone them from our room. This time I planned to say exactly which flight from Innsbruck to Manchester we wanted and to give them a final chance of organising it.

As usual, there was a pause while their operator connected me to the person dealing with our case, during which their company phone played me a tune. It was 'Judas Maccabeus'—well known as the tune for the hymn: 'Thine be the glory'. Usually I just got a couple of lines as they connected me, but for this, my big show-down call, I got two whole verses! Every line, as I sang it out loud down the phone, spoke reassurance to me.

Eventually I was put through. I said, 'You have tried to evade your responsibilities for too long, you don't keep your promises and you refuse to act. Ruth is being discharged from hospital on Wednesday, the funeral is on Friday and we have to travel back to England together. She is not fit enough to drive to Munich as you told us to do. She has to fly from Innsbruck. If you don't make the arrangements today, I'll do it myself and then sue you when I get back to England.'

They capitulated immediately: 'What flight do you want?' I was asked. I told them the flight numbers and they made the arrangements within about an hour. The whole business had soaked up a great deal of nervous energy which could have been used elsewhere. I felt quite drained, but I had fought and won a battle and this had at least restored a little of my damaged self-confidence; and it amused me to think that the company's telephone tune had reminded me of who it was that really had the victory over death and all lesser things!

There was a big improvement in Ruth on the Monday and she was able to start mixing and playing more with the other children. Having her hair washed was another morale booster. She now had company in her room—a boy, Michael, in for a small operation scheduled for his birthday. He started playing with 'Lego'—Matthew's favourite toy. We would be going home to a bedroom full of Matthew's 'Lego' creations, including a half-finished model of the Crich tramway system. We made ourselves take an interest in Michael's 'Lego'—handling it and talking to him about it.

Bereavement has many such hurdles to cross or bogies to defeat. We were discovering that the best way to deal with them was head on. This policy needed courage to carry out but there was the reward of experiencing little victories day by day as we fought our way back to coping with normal life.

Tuesday was a week after the accident—our first anniversary. Christine woke up that morning with a feeling of dread. Then, as she prayed, she realised that, for the first time since the accident, she could say, 'Things won't be as bad today as they were this time last week.' This helped her to look forward rather than back as the day unfolded. It was also good that we were beginning to sleep a little longer at night—perhaps about six hours—and were able to eat more normally.

This was to be our last full day in Austria. We talked during the day about how our lifestyle would have to change and about how we could put a new life together for ourselves. I wondered if I would be able to pick up my interests and hobbies again. Ruth said, 'I'll help you, Dad. I'd like to do bird-watching with you and I could help you with the gardening. I was always more interested in that than Matthew. All he wanted in the garden was a lawn to play football on!'

'Thank you, Ruth,' I said. 'We'll do more things together, you and I. But what about Cambrian House?' (This was our holiday home in Wales which we had bought on moving to theological college, when Ruth was a few weeks old, out of the proceeds of our house in London.) 'It's got such happy memories of times there with Matthew. Could we be happy in it again? Would you like us to keep it or sell it and use the money in another way?'

Ruth thought for a second or two and responded, 'I've had Matthew all my life and I've lost him. I've had Cambrian House all my life and I don't want to lose that as well. It's a lovely holiday house and I'll find things to do by myself when we go.' And so we agreed to keep the house, and I drew strength from the courage and realism with which Ruth was facing the future. It was on this day—Tuesday—that I started to thank God for the blessings I still had in my family, rather than feeling sorry for the blessings lost.

Dr Mayr returned to conduct another neurological examination. Ruth, though trying hard with her walking and getting better each day, was obviously far from right yet. Much to her disgust, the doctor did a thorough examination with his needle and 'donger'. Having a man stick pins in all over her body to find out where it hurt most, was not Ruth's idea of fun!

Dr Mayr's command of technical English was almost perfect, so he was able to dictate a report to me for a neurologist in England. I then

typed this up on the ward typewriter. A German
language typewriter was quite a challenge, as the
letters were in different places, with the 'z' firmly in
the middle where it belonged—being a common
character in German. Even though we knew Dr
Mayr only slightly, we chatted like old friends and
he invited us to stay at his house should we ever
return to Austria. We in turn invited him to stay
with us in England. He had an ambition to walk the
Pennine Way, although I wasn't convinced that he
realised how many waterproofs he would need for
the trip! The combination of medical treatment
and personal consideration given to us could not
have been faulted, and we were to leave Austria
with bittersweet memories of the hills but an un-
mixed warm regard for the people.

The next day, armed with computer tomography photos and English and German medical
reports, we were ready to leave. Ruth's main
medical report was still in German and we had
arranged for a friend in Sheffield, a medical
professor, to have it translated there. In the morning I had to go to the medical records office to sign
Ruth out of hospital. While I was away there
occurred our first and only communication break-
down caused by the language barrier. Ruth had
gone to the toilet that morning but hadn't told this
to the nurses. They were determined to empty her
bowels before she had to travel. So before the poor
girl realised what was happening to her they gave
her an enema! But the incident made us reflect that
many such misunderstandings *could* have occurred
and appreciate the fact that they *hadn't*.

The taxi, ordered to take us to the airport,

never arrived, so one of the doctors drove us at high speed through the city in her own car—a final act of kindness. We caught the plane—just! Jonathan was there to wave us off and we were on our way at last, flying first with Tyrolean Airways to Frankfurt and then with Lufthansa to Manchester. Lufthansa were most efficient in organising a wheelchair and ambulance to convey Ruth across the many acres of Frankfurt airport, and a wheel-chair for her at Ringway. Sue and Christine, having gone the long way round, arrived exhausted and only just in time for the plane at Frankfurt. They found a happy Ruth sharing her seat with sweets and dolls.

'Where did you get those from, Ruth?' gasped Christine.

'The stewardess gave them to me,' came back the answer. So Ruth had a happy flight home.

As we landed at Ringway, Christine held my hand and said, 'I don't know what it holds, but this is the beginning of the future. This is where it all starts. It'll need lots of courage but the Lord's in it and we'll be all right.'

Several friends from church, as well as Sue's family, were there to meet us. They needed courage too as they wondered apprehensively how we would be. After a short, emotional reunion with them, Christine, Ruth and I boarded a South Yorkshire Ambulance that took us along the Woodhead Pass and over the Pennine Way back towards Grenoside and home.

Richard and Gill Sheldon—a young couple from church, who had gone forward, as had Matthew and Ruth, in response to Billy Graham's appeal the previous summer—followed us in their car, which also carried our luggage. We nearly lost them once. The ambulance stopped at a busy roundabout to let Ruth lie down, and then sped off again, just as Richard was out of the car to see what the matter was! But in the end, we all made it safely home.

The thought of being reunited with Sam, our well-meaning but slightly dim Golden Retriever, had helped to sustain Ruth in hospital. I had arranged for him to be home from the kennels to meet us as we arrived and he greeted us in his usual ecstatic way and was to prove a loyal and important friend to us in our new situation. He was someone to love and to keep us amused in the familiar yet strangely empty environment of home.

Other friends from church were also at home to welcome us. The strange fear of meeting again for the first time soon evaporated in the atmosphere of care and friendliness. The garden had been tidied, the house cleaned up, and tea prepared for us. Ruth was presented with an enormous teddy bear from the church, bought out of a love gift collected the previous Sunday. Its size and cuddliness reminded Ruth irresistibly of her friendly surgeon in Innsbruck, and so she immediately christened it 'Hager'.

Just before leaving the *Klinik* in Innsbruck, one of the nurses had mustered up her English and said to me, 'You have had a very strong week.' I had realised immediately that she had mistranslated a German word—*schwer*—which can mean either 'strong' or 'difficult'. I had explained, and we had agreed that it had been a difficult week.

But Christine had said, 'You know, she was right the first time. We have had an amazingly strong week.' In our time of trial and torment we had been strong in the strength which God supplies through his eternal Son. Weak in ourselves, we had been made strong by the God of all strength and comfort.

We would need him to go on making us strong in the times that lay ahead.

5
Home—with a difference

The visitors came in a constant stream for our first few days back home. So many family, friends, and church people were grieving almost as deeply as we were. They needed to see us and hold us. Above all they needed our testimony of faith to be strong. We realised that our week in Innsbruck had been a time of preparation and strengthening for this task.

Our friends had not been idle while we had been away. They had held their Memorial Service for Matthew. Tim Gregory had shouldered the task of being a leader and inspiration for the congregation. There were flowers and presents for us all. There were also about two hundred cards and letters waiting for us, and many hundreds more were to come through our letter-box in the weeks which followed. Some wrote movingly, enclosing verses and poems, or describing their own experiences of losing a child; other simply sent cards. But all were a strength and comfort to us: tangible evidence of the vast network of prayer and concern that we had felt sustaining us in Innsbruck.

There was one full day after arriving home before Matthew's funeral. In the morning the coroner's office rang to ask me to come straight down for an inquest. I understood that the inquest would be opened formally, to allow the funeral to take place, and resumed a few weeks later. But in the event it was completed on that day.

The doctor who had conducted the *post mortem* gave evidence first.

'Is it in order to ask questions?' I enquired of the coroner. He replied in the affirmative so I asked the doctor, 'I think I understood what you said, but could you tell me directly—did Matthew die instantly from his fall?'

'Yes he did,' the doctor replied. My 'thank you' was heartfelt. Gone was the guilty fear that I might have saved Matthew's life on the mountainside, if only I had had the necessary medical knowledge. Gone too was the thought that if help had arrived more quickly, this would have made a difference.

I was then sworn in and the coroner said, 'Could you tell me all you know about exactly what happened?' I had told the story so many times to our visitors that I managed to tell it fairly fluently— all the while very aware of the fact that behind me, in the public gallery, were two rows of reporters, taking down in shorthand all I was saying. The story was clearly going to be in the national papers again the next day, the day of the funeral.

On my way out of the court I spoke to the reporters: 'Please keep your stories as toned down as possible. I'm thinking of our daughter. She was upset when she knew the story had been in the papers last week, in case people thought she was to blame for not rescuing Matthew, even though she held on to him so long she was dragged over herself.'

'We'll do our best,' answered one—apparently nearly in tears himself. 'But the story will be syndicated and we can't control how the different papers will alter it.'

'Could you tell us where and when the funeral is?' asked another. I replied, 'No—I'd prefer to keep the funeral private.'

We prayed for protection from the media when I got home. The coverage on television that night and in the papers next morning was fairly factual. Only one or two tabloids made a real meal of it. In case any reporters or cameramen should turn up at the funeral, I arranged for Percy Hanson, a Special Constabulary Superintendent, who was also one of our church members, to be on duty outside the church.

Our funeral director, Ann Heward, was another friend and church member. She had the job of making all our arrangements while coping with her own emotions. Apparently, the Austrian Death Certificate was needed before the funeral could take place but this had gone missing some-where around the coroner's office. Though only minutes away on the Friday morning from having to cancel the funeral for lack of paperwork, Ann never burdened us with this problem. In fact, she sorted things out just in time.

Normal sensible advice is never to lead or speak at the funeral service of someone very close, because trying to keep composed is too much of a strain, and because, at such times, the bereaved need someone else's ministry. Nevertheless, ever since Christine's threatened miscarriage I had always expected to speak at Matthew's funeral, and so I was sure that God wanted me to do it.

Six years previously, while we had been at St John's College training for the Ministry, the wife of Alan, one of my fellow-students had died quite quickly of cancer, leaving him with four young children. His faith and strength had been an inspiration to everyone. His face had seemed to shine with a great radiance rather like Moses' face when he had met the Lord face to face.

At the funeral service in the college chapel, Alan had read the whole of 1 Corinthians 15—that great chapter on the resurrection faith of Christians—with rock solid power and conviction. The service had contained not only grief and loss but also faith and victory.

'If God could do that for Alan, he can do it for me,' I thought. 'He wants me to speak so he will give me the courage and strength to get the words out with conviction.'

The funeral of a child can be so bleak and hopeless, but we were determined that Matthew's funeral should not be either, because we had Christian hope.

I began to thank God, as the funeral approached, that I had become a Christian, twenty years earlier, through being convinced of the historical truth of Jesus' resurrection. Many children begin life with a faith which they reject as they grow up. I never had a faith to reject. God and eternity were unreal to me from the start. I never stumbled across God round the street corner, and the comforts of religion seemed to me to be the wish fulfilment of the weak-minded. Heaven was just a nice thought. God had been created by man to meet his own needs. This clear-minded certainty I maintained through years at Sunday School and then at a Crusader Bible Class at Bents Green Methodist Church near my parents' home in Sheffield. The Bible Class attracted me by its football and camping and the caring qualities of its leaders, rather than by its religious teaching.

Then, one Sunday, our Bible Class went through the evidence for the resurrection. At sixteen, I understood how unlikely the alternative explanations for the disappearance of Jesus' body sounded. I realised how inexplicable the behaviour of the disciples would have been had they not genuinely believed in the resurrected Jesus. I accepted that something extraordinary must have happened to trigger the explosive growth of the first Christian Church. I knew that Jesus had predicted it all before his death. For the first time in my life I was made to face the possibility that my simple childhood certainties were wrong. I walked out of the Crusader Class that day thinking, 'Goodness, what if it's all true after all?' Over the next few months my pride and resistence crumbled until I came to accept that Jesus certainly did rise from the dead.

I knew the logical consequences of accepting the resurrection. If Jesus had risen, his claim to be God's only Son would have been authenticated. An imposter couldn't have been resurrected. Jesus'

promise that those who trusted him would defeat
death too, would have to be accepted. He was alive
today and I could pray to him and build a relationship with him in the present. Everything flowed
from accepting the resurrection; I agreed with St
Paul about that:

> If Christ has not been raised, our preaching is use-
> less and so is your faith . . . If Christ has not been
> raised, your faith is futile; you are still in your sins.
> Then those who also have fallen asleep in Christ
> are lost. If only for this life we have hope in Christ,
> we are to be pitied more than all men. But Christ
> has indeed been raised from the dead, the first-
> fruits of those who have fallen asleep (1
> Corinthians 15:14, 17–20).

If Jesus' resurrection hadn't happened what
hope was there for lesser mortals? In that case I
would have had to face the fact that Matthew was
dead and gone; that it was as though he had never
existed; and that one day it would be the same for
me. But if Jesus had torn a way through the curtain
of death for us to follow, then a whole new reality
had been opened up, and the whole of life transformed:

> 'If the dead are not raised, "Let us eat and drink,
> for tomorrow we die" . . . [But:] Death has been
> swallowed up in victory . . . [So:] Always give your-
> selves fully to the work of the Lord, because you
> know that your labour in the Lord is not in vain' (1
> Corinthians 15:32,54,58).

Without my twenty-year belief in the resurrection, I would have been defeated; with it I had
hope, courage and victory. One day I would be

with Matthew and remain with him for eternity. All I had and held on to was invested in my faith in the resurrection of Jesus and, therefore, of Matthew.

As I dressed on the morning of the funeral—not in black but in new clothes of the style and colour range that I usually wore—I thanked God from the depths of my heart that the resurrection was the solid foundation stone of my faith. I promised him that I would give the rest of my life fully to his work and knew that it would not be in vain.

When his son had died, King David had said:

> 'Now that he is dead, why should I fast? Can I bring him back again? I will go to him, but he will not return to me' (2 Samuel 12:23).

This combination of resignation ('I will go to him') and despair ('he will not return to me') has been echoed in the deep sighs of grieving parents through the ages. David, a man of his times, did not have a full or comforting picture of the after-life. Instead he envisaged the shadowy, grey half-life of Sheol. As a Christian I echoed David's comments but my emotions were different. Instead of mere resignation there was my anticipation of heaven; instead of despairing sorrow, there was sorrow shot through with hope.

> Brothers, we do not want you to be ignorant about those who fall asleep, or to grieve like the rest of men, who have no hope. We believe that Jesus died and rose again and so we believe that God will bring with Jesus those who have fallen asleep in him (1 Thessalonians 4:13,14).

In planning the service, our aim was to try to meet people where they were—in the depths—and then raise them, in hope and triumph with Matthew, to the throne of heaven.

Grief and hope were battling for supremacy in my mind as I played 'Thine be the glory' on the piano, while waiting for Ann Heward to arrive with her cars and take us the short distance to St Mark's. Vicarage phones don't stop ringing whatever happens, and Christine, at the time, was coping with a call from a rather incoherent Jehovah's Witness. She found the grace to be polite to him— and felt thankful for the solid biblical basis of her Christian faith, which was able to support her in her time of need. She ended the call and, the cars having arrived, we left for church.

6
A Christian funeral

St Mark's was packed. There were extra chairs in
every nook and cranny of the church as well as in
the hall—which was wired up in readiness for the
overflow. Ruth was still walking with difficulty and
the stitches near the base of her spine had not yet
been removed. We sat on chairs in front of the
front pew, with Ruth on a cushion. Although it was
impossible to take note of all who were present, we
felt completely surrounded by the love, concern
and shared grief of our family and friends; and the
media didn't intrude, for which we were thankful.

We were very pleased that the Bishop of
Doncaster, Bill Persson, had agreed to take the
service. He and Matthew had swapped little jokes
and riddles whenever they had met. On the last
occasion, the Bishop had come to tea prior to a
confirmation service, and—much to our amusement—Matthew had memorised for his benefit an
immensely long question-and-answer joke with
Ruth.

We were touched, too, when the Bishop of

Sheffield, David Lunn, asked if he might take part as well; and it was he who led us into church with the sentences of Scripture that preface the funeral service in the modern prayer book. Many of these had become particularly precious to us in the previous ten days. John Shaw, the organist, played the tune of, 'Do not be worried and upset.'

The Bishop of Doncaster announced the first hymn and we sang:

> *How sweet the name of Jesus sounds*
> *In a believer's ear!*
> *It soothes his sorrows, heals his wounds,*
> *And drives away his fear.*

Jesus had not waved a magic wand and taken our sorrows, wounds and fears away; rather he had identified with them and was tending them (and us) like a good nurse or doctor—making wounded spirits whole and calming troubled breasts.

After the hymn, the whole church read out loud together Psalm 23. We were in the valley of the shadow of death but we could begin to say with David that we would fear no evil because God's rod and staff were comforting us.

I then went to the front to do the main Bible reading—partly to get my voice going before I spoke, but mostly because I wanted to offer Jesus' words of comfort to my grieving family and friends.

'Do not be worried and upset,' Jesus told them. 'Believe in God and believe also in me. There are many rooms in my Father's house, and I am going to prepare a place for you. I would not tell you this if it were not so. And after I go and prepare a place for you, I will come back and take you to myself, so that you will be where I am. You know the way that leads to the place where I am going.' Thomas said to him, 'Lord, we do not know where you are going; so how can we know the way to get there?' Jesus answered him, 'I am the way, the truth, and the life; no one goes to the Father except by me. Now that you have known me,' he said to them, 'you will know my Father also, and from now on you do know him and have seen him . . . Peace is what I leave with you; it is my own peace that I give you. I do not give it as the world does. Do not be worried and upset; do not be afraid. You heard me say to you, "I am leaving, but I will come back to you." If you loved me, you would be glad that I am going to the Father; for he is greater than I. I have told you this now before it all happens, so that when it does happen, you will believe' (John 14:1–6,27–29 TEV).

I had prepared notes of what to say, but didn't really stick to them. After thanking everyone for all their prayers and support, I told them how God had warned us that we would lose Matthew even before he was born. It was why I had included verse 29 in the reading—'I have told you this now before it happens, so that, when it does happen, you will believe.' I talked about how we felt Matthew was a very special gift from God to us. He had known Jesus as his Saviour and had had a wonderfully full and happy life right up to the day of his accident.

'The day before,' I continued, 'we had been on chair-lifts over a glacier to the top of a very high mountain. The day had been glorious, and at the end of it, Matthew said to us that it had been the best and happiest day of his life. And as we prayed together, as we often did in the evening, he very earnestly thanked God for the beauty of his world. Matthew died full of happiness and full of trust in Jesus. And that means everything to me because I've always had the feeling that one day God would ask me to speak at Matthew's funeral, which is what I'm doing now.'

Then I said that there were three things I wanted to say to everyone. The first was that what mattered in life was not how long we lived but whether we had put our trust in God and his Son, because heaven was our real and eternal home. Matthew, I said, was now with God in heaven. I went on, 'All his potential is not wasted but will be fulfilled in heaven where God now has something very special for him to do. So, although we grieve for ourselves, we rejoice for him; and I pray that you will rejoice with us for Matthew this day.'

The second thing was that I wanted all of them to be ready for death, just as Matthew had been. I added, 'I want to ask all of you not to be worried and upset but to trust in God still and to trust in Jesus. And, as we face the ultimate things together here this morning, do bring your doubts and your questions as Thomas did in the reading we had. But also bring your trust to Jesus Christ and trust him with your life, to be your way through life and then through the valley of the shadow of death into the dawn of eternity.'

'And finally,' I said, 'many of you have said, "Is there anything we can do? How can we help you?" I want to say there is a way to help us very much and this is it. We hope and believe that many people's lives have been affected by what happened. I know of some problems healed, and of one or two people whose lives have grown closer to the Lord over the last week. This is how you can help us—by writing to us or talking to us and letting us know what's happened with you and between you and God. We want the encouragement of knowing that God has brought people closer to himself through what has happened. That would be a great help to us. That's how you can help us—talking to us or writing to us over the weeks to come.'

Then I asked them to go on praying for us and assured them again that their prayers were being answered. Finally I said that Ruth had told us not to have any 'down in the dumps music'. As well as our human sorrow, there should also be triumph in the air when a Christian goes to be with the Lord, so we would sing two of Matthew's favourite songs.

First, we sang the chorus that Matthew had sung so often round the house to the 'Match of the Day' tune, the truth of which he had, we believed, experienced himself:

Why don't you put your trust in Jesus and follow Christ the King?
Why don't you serve the living Jesus, you owe him everything?
Why don't you give your life to Jesus and make a brand new start?
Life is rich and full beyond compare with Jesus in your heart!

As we sang, Christine and I prayed that there might be people in the congregation who would respond to those questions, put their trust in Jesus and give us some positive joy to put alongside our sorrow. We then sang the song, 'Majesty, worship his majesty,' before Harry Birkby, our church secretary, read Psalm 91, as requested by Ruth. Harry's clear voice was only slightly less steady than usual.

Then the Bishop of Doncaster ascended the pulpit steps and spoke to us. Up to this point the service had been our offering to the other mourners. Now it was our turn simply to receive. The Bishop took as his text:

I looked, and lo, in heaven an open door! (Revelation 4:1 RSV).

He echoed what I had said in wanting to thank God for the gift of Matthew—whom he described as such an intelligent and lively boy with a simple but mature trust in Jesus. He had thought of Matthew as being, in a way, his son—was well as ours—because of the relationship they had had, and he was grieving with us, he said. But, he went on, as a consequence of the tragedy, our church folk would have a deeper and fuller ministry to us and we to them, and God would bless our ministry in the parish in a new and remarkable way.

He spoke of the fact that at night we lock our front doors and turn out the lights, but in the morning we open our doors and the light of a new day streams into the house. He said that in a time of loss we tend to feel that it's evening, and the door is shut, and the light has gone out. But

actually, it's morning, because the door is opened.
If we look through it we see the one who sits on the
throne, the saints and angels and all the glory of
heaven, and Matthew eternally praising and serving God. That door is open, he said, because Jesus
has opened it for all who trust in his death and
resurrection. It's always open, he told us, so we
should not be earthbound but rather look in
heaven's direction through the open door to see
Matthew at his Saviour's side; and, when we do
this, we will find that really it's the Saviour—Jesus
Christ our friend—at whom we are looking,
together with Matthew.

The picture of heaven's open door has stuck
with us ever since, and we now pray for glimpses
through it to sustain us on our journey there. Unlike Matthew, we are having to walk the long way
round.

Tim Gregory prayed for us in his usual
sensitive way and we sang a final hymn of triumph
over death:

> I am the resurrection,
> I am the life.
> He who believes in me,
> Even if he die, he shall live for ever.
> And I will raise him up,
> And I will raise him up,
> And I will raise him up,
> On the last day.

The Bishop of Sheffield gave the blessing.
Then, as we began to process out behind the coffin,
John Shaw began to play, 'Thine be the glory'. Sue,
remembering the phone calls from Innsbruck,

whispered to us, 'They are playing our tune!' As we
filed out of our seats the congregation began to
pick up the words, singing softly at first, then
rising, as we moved outside, to a crescendo which
billowed out of the open door:

> *Lo! Jesus meets us, risen from the tomb;*
> *Lovingly he greets us, scatters fear and gloom;*
> *Let the Church with gladness hymns of triumph sing,*
> *For her Lord now liveth; death hast lost its sting.*
> *Thine be the glory, risen, conquering Son,*
> *Endless is the victory Thou o'er death hast won.*

Matthew's friends and instructors from St
John Ambulance were lined up outside as a guard
of honour for him—a tribute which, for the first
time that morning, brought tears to all our eyes.

It was a long drive to the committal, at City
Road Cemetery in Sheffield, where I had once
been an assistant grave-digger as a student seventeen years earlier, and where I now often take
funerals. On the ride, it occurred to me that any
fear of death and dying that I had once had, was
gone completely. I had resented encroaching
middle age and lost youthfulness; that resentment
was gone. Growing old was to be my route to
Matthew and to Jesus, so I would grow old gladly.
Death had truly lost its sting for me and become my
friend. There was much to do in the meantime, but
I felt I could truly say with St Paul that to me to live
was Christ and to die was gain.

Many of the children came with us to the
graveside and were able to look down at the coffin
and be fully involved. We felt that this was a good
thing and that it might help them to overcome

some of their own fears of funerals, of death and dying, as well as enabling them to grieve properly and adjust to life without Matthew.

About two days after Matthew's death I had been walking back to the *Klinik* very early in the morning to catch Ruth waking up, when the thought had come to me that there might be a book to write about our experience of losing Matthew. I had said nothing to Christine, but when she had begun her diary of events a day or two later, the same thought had occurred to her. We could see many problems, not least for Ruth, in making our private experience public and in having to go over every painful experience again. On the other hand, writing everything down might help us to see and remember the hand of God in events. Also it might clarify our questions and problems and help our friends and family to understand all that we wanted to share with them.

However, I was afraid of the task of writing a book and resolved only to consider it if someone else independently suggested it. That made me feel pretty safe! But as we walked away from Matthew's grave after the committal, Richard Sheldon, who had driven our luggage back from the airport, blurted out to me, 'I think you ought to write a book about this, you know. People would find it very helpful.' I made some lame excuse and he repeated himself enthusiastically, though I was not sure he knew why! After that several others made the same suggestion, but it was Richard's words at Matthew's graveside that confirmed for me the idea that God was giving me the task of writing a book.

7
Where is Matthew now?

In the weeks following the funeral many Christian friends expressed their deep appreciation of the strength of our resurrection faith shown in the funeral service. Too often all Christians can muster is, 'Lord I believe, help thou my unbelief.' A colleague recently conducted a survey of his own congregation and found that, though they all believed Jesus to be the Son of God, little more than half of them believed in life after death for themselves. This is quite illogical, for why would the Son of God lie to us about heaven? But, then, illogicality has never seriously bothered the average human mind!

Not many Christians, I believe, come to faith, as I did, by becoming convinced of the resurrection. Often it's a sense of need and guilt or the attractiveness of a church fellowship that draws them in; or a sense of God and his goodness. Nowadays in Britain many people can live for years without having to face up to the realities of death and bereavement, or questions about resurrection and eternity. This was not so true for our forebears nor is it so for Christians living in the Third World. But in the West it sometimes takes a big shock like the death of a child to make many wake up to eternity. When something like that happens, Christians may find themselves feeling very unsure about their belief in resurrection—something they haven't thought much about or had put to the test.

Naturally, we had our own doubts and fears both on the day of the funeral and subsequently, Christine's mind told her that Matthew was in heaven. But her emotions raised all sorts of fearful questions. What if Matthew had only play-acted his faith and had secretly rejected it? Would he be with God then? She felt such fears to be alien and mischievous but they still came to haunt her. She found that God wanted her to use her mind properly and face up to problems. A well-thought-out faith would withstand the pressure at a time when her emotions would continue to be erratic. So over the months, she worked through her beliefs, reviewing her Christian faith against all the alternatives.

She emerged with her faith confirmed—convinced in particular of Jesus' resurrection, and of the reality of life after death.

But how could she be sure that Matthew was in heaven rather than in that separation from God which we know as hell? Logically, she knew he must be in heaven, but so much was at stake that she had to feel almost ridiculously sure of it. She ended up by making two lists—one with reasons for doubting and the other with reasons for believing that Matthew was in heaven. There were two rather dubious reasons in the first list and fourteen solid ones in the second. This she found to be a great help.

The thought which haunted me was: What if God and resurrection are just comfortable illusions after all? Against this I could set my twenty years' experience of the living God. Surely I had not been relating to a mirage all that time! In this test of my faith, my past experience was vitally important to me. If I had come to God 'cold' in my crisis I wouldn't have had the reassurance of that past experience. As it was, my relatively calm, un-troubled years had been used to build a solid foundation on the rock of the risen Christ. When the sudden storm broke, I had no time to sink a new foundation: it was the old one that held. Yet I still had to battle with the thought that faith in heaven for Matthew was too good to be true. Was it any more than a convenient belief which my mind needed to keep it sane and to cope with grief?

I was helped by remembering that most societies have a belief in the after-life, but not always a very pleasant one. The last steam engine ran on British Rail in 1968. But for many years afterwards some survivors have stood rusting away in scrap-yards in South Wales—for ever cold, silent, helpless parodies of their former selves. To me that conjures up Sheol—the after-life imagined in the early Old Testament period. Wherever that idea came from, it can hardly have been the result of wishful thinking! It seems that man, out of all God's creatures, not only knows that he is going to die but also senses eternity in his heart; he has a sense of destiny which cannot be explained by life in this world or by wishful thinking about the next. I could not believe that the life within Matthew could have been snuffed out simply by physical death. Also Christians believe that God has brought us all into being in order that he should enjoy our company and that we should enjoy his. So it was inconceivable that he would discard us at death, before our destiny of fellowship with him could be properly achieved.

A couple of weeks after the funeral, Ruth was in bed reading when I came to turn her light out.

'Dad, how can we know that Matthew is in heaven with Jesus?' she asked. I sat on the bed, took a deep breath and got as far as saying, 'Firstly . . .'—intending to say that we knew Jesus rose because his friends saw him. But Ruth promptly answered her own question by saying, 'Because God and Matthew have spoken to me.'

We talked about some of the other ways in which God had helped us in recent weeks—through Bible verses, through prayer and through remembering our warning about Matthew. I told Ruth about Christine's last lesson with the boys in her Explorer Group before we'd gone away. It had been based on John chapter 14 verses 1 to 6—about Jesus being the way to his Father's house—the passage I had read at Matthew's funeral. Christine had put up on the overhead projector the words which Matthew had once said as a small child: 'When we go to heaven, Mummy, you two can walk but Jesus will carry me.' She hadn't told the group who had said this—and ten-year-old Matthew, in his corner, had kept quiet about it. We agreed that it was remarkable that Christine had remembered and used that incident in view of how soon Matthew was to experience the 'carry' he had spoken about. In the same lesson, Christine had taught the boys a song, 'Soon and very soon we are going to see the King.' Matthew had really taken to the song and in the last two weeks of his life had gone around singing it everywhere.

'We'll all see the King soon,' I said to Ruth, 'but for Matthew it was very soon. That's why I'm finding it a comfort to play the song on the piano so much at the moment. God gave it to us and to Matthew to reassure us about Matthew being in heaven.'

The day we began to sort out Matthew's bedroom was not an easy one. We packed away his toys and clothes and took down his certificates and posters from the walls. The clothes were to go to Margaret Cranston, our missionary friend in Nepal, for clothing some of the boys in her school. The toys and certificates were destined for the loft. Tears ran down my face as I accumulated the adhesive from the cheerful mixture of railway photographs and Christian posters which had covered Matthew's walls. I felt as though I were dismantling an expression of Matthew's personality, destroying something that was intimately his. We now realised why some bereaved parents keep a child's room unchanged as a sort of shrine to him or her. It's an unhealthy thing to do, but understandable.

As I worked and wept, Christine said, 'Don't be upset, Matthew's got a much better room than this now.' She was thinking of John chapter 14 again and of Jesus' promise: 'In my Father's house are many rooms.' As I, his earthly father, dismantled Matthew's room in my house, it was a great help to realise that he now had his own room in his heavenly Father's house.

As well as all that had to be done in connection with Matthew's death, I had my church work. One job was to write my monthly letter in the church magazine, which sold 1,200 copies around the parish. I sat down to do this a week after the funeral. First, I checked what I had written about in the previous two months—before we'd gone away.

In the June letter I had referred to the accident to the Russian nuclear power station at Chernobyl, and posed the question, 'What has a Christian got to say when people are killed in accidents?' My answer had been that most accidents have obvious human causes and cannot be blamed on God; even so, he identifies with human suffering in his Son and redeems it through the cross.

In July, I had mentioned the local celebrations of the 900th anniversary of the Domesday Book, and reflected on the words: 'A thousand years in your sight are like a day that has just gone by' (Psalm 90:4). The letter had ended by saying, 'For Christians today it is in our common worship of the unchanging Saviour, in our common adherence to the same Gospel and Creed, in our common experience of the Holy Spirit, that is found our close affinity with those who lived and worshipped here 900 years ago. Our brief lives find their eternal importance in their unique place in the tapestry of Christian history which God is weaving in his world. We need such a sense of history to know the greatness of the timeless God and our part in his plans as they unfold for the future.'

I had never written on such themes as coping with accidental death, and the brevity of life before. Surely, Christine and I felt, these were subjects which God had given me to write on, so that the truths I expressed from before my bereavement could minister to us now. Matthew's life had indeed been brief, but he would have a unique and important place in the tapestry of history which God was weaving. We could not see yet its context in the completed work, but we could perhaps begin to discern parts in close up.

There were some other strange happenings about which we reflected. One of these was the fact that Terry Jones, our Baptist friend with whom we'd stayed in Ashford before going to Mayrhofen, had written to us on the day of Matthew's funeral: 'Just a few days before Matthew's death we' (referring to himself and his church deacons) 'were speaking together about the place of suffering in the ministry and Christian experience, and, in a strange way, confirmed by events, we felt that you might soon face such a situation.'

Christine and I didn't really know what to make of such things. But perhaps they were God's way of preparing us and others for Matthew's death and of helping us to see his activity surrounding it.

It was very good to remember Matthew singing, 'Soon and very soon,' and to remind ourselves that he'd called his last full day on earth the best day of his life and that he'd been talking about heaven with Ruth up to the moment of his fall. We reflected on his last words, 'I'll fall but you'll be all right,' and wondered if he had known that his time had come. I remembered wondering the same, a long time before, about a friend who had drowned while out canoeing. He had been at a Crusader houseparty on the Isle of Wight at the time and, the previous evening, had spoken powerfully about the importance of being right with Jesus because we never know when our lives will end. Whether or not he or Matthew had any inkling of their imminent deaths, we couldn't be sure. But we *did* believe that God had given my friend the right message for the circumstances just as he'd filled Matthew's mind with heaven as a preparation for him and a reassurance for us.

Christine and I also talked about our feeling, while waiting to see Matthew's body, of being admitted to the fellowship of Christ's sufferings. The path along which the four of us had walked on the afternoon of Matthew's accident, commemorates the Stations of the Cross—the stages through which Christ had gone in his crucifixion ordeal. At each bend of this path is a large crucifix and beyond the last one stands a tiny chapel. Thinking back to this, I could not get it out of my mind that our son had been killed while we'd been walking the Stations of the Cross; and Christine found herself identifying with Mary, Jesus' mother, as she had had the painful privilege of walking her *Via Dolorosa*. This was just another detail of our story which, when we'd reflected on it, awed and reassured us.

Among the hundreds of special letters waiting for us on our return from Innsbruck was my usual vicar's mail. It included a report called, 'The Nature of Christian Belief'. This, published the week Matthew died, was the Bishops' collective and official response to the controversies stirred up by the Bishop of Durham. Its longest and most important chapter was about the resurrection of Jesus—a subject in which I now had a deep personal interest. Would the Bishops say that Jesus really had risen or that resurrection was simply a way the disciples had found to describe the continuing influence of their late lamented friend? In fact, the report clearly reasserted a traditional straightforward faith in the Resurrection:

> We believe that Jesus' Resurrection was something that happened, regardless of observers, narrators or believers. Jesus truly died and was buried, and as truly rose again to eternal life . . . We believe in the Resurrection as 'something that happened', something to which faith was a response, not something which faith created.

It helped me to know that what I believed was still the official teaching of the Anglican church.

But Christine and I were concerned to work out, as far as we could, the details of that belief in resurrection life in heaven. Many questions rose in our minds.

The first was, 'Has Matthew's resurrection life already begun? Is he in heaven now?' The answer we reached was, 'Yes,' and our reasoning went something like this:

When he was on the cross, Jesus promised to the penitent thief, 'Today you will be with me in paradise' (Luke 23:43). Paul also implies an immediate translation from earth to heaven in his letter to the Philippians. Just as Matthew had done moments before his death, Paul wondered whether it was better to remain alive or to go to heaven:

> For to me to live is Christ and to die is gain . . . Yet what shall I choose? I do not know! I am torn between the two: I desire to depart and be with Christ, which is better by far (Philippians 1:21–23).

True, the Bible speaks of resurrection 'at the last day' (John 6:40), but also of it happening 'in a flash, in the twinkling of an eye' (1 Corinthians 15:52). Unlike some fringe sects, mainstream Christianity does not embrace the idea of souls sleeping until the end of the world. If there were such a sleep, the communion of saints would not be a reality. The dilemma, we believe, arises from the fact that time and space are both dimensions of our own created order, whereas heaven is beyond space and time as we know them. We came to the conclusion that it was logical as well as scriptural to think of Matthew as having stepped outside our space and time into another reality 'in the twinkling of an eye'. As we look at heaven from our present, Matthew is already there. When we pray to the eternal God, Matthew is with him in his timeless eternity.

A second question was, 'But what is heaven like?' That's not easy to answer because the Bible doesn't give us a clear, detailed picture of heaven— perhaps partly because we wouldn't be able to comprehend such a picture: visualising an

existence outside time is mind-boggling, for a start!
As St Paul rightly says:

> No eye has seen, no ear has heard,
> no mind has conceived what God has prepared for
> those who love him (1 Corinthians 2:9).

Nevertheless, we are not without help. The
following verse says, 'But God has revealed it to us
by his Spirit.' God's Spirit can help us see the
realities of heaven. We can, as the Bishop said at
Matthew's funeral, peer with the writer of
Revelation through heaven's open door and see,
not everything, but a little:

> Now we see but a poor reflection as in a mirror;
> then we shall see face to face. Now I know in part;
> then I shall know fully, even as I am fully known (1
> Corinthians 13:12).

Recognising that we can only know 'in part',
Christine and I reflected on what Christians can
know about heaven. We knew that Matthew would
have found heaven to be familiar, not strange. The
Bible does not talk about 'going away to heaven
when we die', but about a transformed, perfected
universe—a new heaven and a new earth:

> The creation itself will be liberated from its
> bondage to decay and brought into the glorious
> freedom of the children of God (Romans 8:21).

Matthew will have found his new world to be
no less real than his old one; and not alien and
frightening, but truly his natural home. It will be
like the best of this earth with none of the negative
things – no decay or evil; no insecurities, fears or

uncertainties; no death or grief or crying or pain or suffering:

> For the Lamb at the centre of the throne will be their shepherd;
> he will lead them to springs of living water.
> And God will wipe away every tear from their eyes
> There will be no more death or mourning or crying or pain, for the old order of things has passed away (Revelation 7:17;21:4).

It follows, too, that Matthew will have retained his individual identity and that he will recognise others and they will recognise him. There will be no mystical absorption of the individual into God; no collective consciousness. That would not tally with Jesus referring to named individuals from Israel's past as being in the Kingdom of Heaven—Abraham, Isaac and Jacob (Matthew 8:11). Jesus himself after his resurrection was still recognisable as the same individual, even though his glorified body needed a second or third glance to be identified. This might have been, partly, because a resurrection body is —presumably—of no particular age. In heaven Matthew is no more aged ten than Jesus is thirty-three or than Matthew's great grandad is ninety-six—the age at which he died.

Jesus is equally clear that not everyone will find their way to heaven: those who reject him, reject their chance of heaven:

> Whoever believes in the Son has eternal life, but whoever rejects the Son will not see life, for God's wrath remains on him (John 3:36).

But for those, like Matthew, who trust themselves to Jesus, heaven will be a wonderful place of reunions and first meetings. People from every tribe, language, nation, race and time—all those who love the Lord—will be there, including, very specially for us, our Matthew; including, too, one of the older ladies at St Mark's, a lovely saint called Alma with whom Matthew had been friendly. Alma died a few months after Matthew and both her family and ours felt that though we had lost Alma, Matthew had gained her.

Heaven, though not wholly unlike earth, will be far better. Matthew had potential on earth but we will never know what would have happened to him had he lived. His potential in heaven is far greater. There are also things he has been spared. He will never know the loss of happiness, health or faith. Teenage traumas will never trouble him; adult neuroses will not come near him; his joints will never creak with age. He has been spared the horrors of brain damage, life-support machines and wheel-chairs, which might have been necessary if he had been severely injured instead of killed. For Matthew this life had indeed been 'rich and full beyond compare with Jesus in his heart' until the day when he was quickly carried to his heavenly life which is far, far better. So there is no need to feel sorry for Matthew because he had such a short life on earth; such sorrow simply shows lack of faith in the character and reality of heaven.

The problem of how Matthew's human potential could be utilised and realised in heaven is complicated by the popular image of heaven being populated by dreamboats, riding clouds and

strumming harps—never forming an orchestra
and having nothing in particular to do. If heaven is
to house fulfilled human beings, it must—we
think—be a place where effort, creativity and
achievement are possible. God made man in his
own image and likeness and God is a worker. He
worked in creation, and works today in the sustaining of his universe. Adam, the prototype man
made in God's image, was a worker too—creatively
tending the Garden of Eden before things went
wrong. Our drive to work, create and achieve
would seem to be central to the concept of a
perfectly restored humanity in heaven.

The resurrection appearances of Jesus show
that the transition to heaven will be made with a
continuity of character and personhood. In heaven
we will be truly and perfectly the people we were
meant to be. Achievement of potential, fulfilment
in creativity, and the work of loving and serving
others will be even more the stuff of abundant
living for Matthew perfected in heaven than they
were for Matthew imperfect on earth. All of his
energy, enthusiasm, ability and love of life are even
now being channelled into the glorious, creative
service of heaven's community of love.

Heaven must be a place not of endless same-
ness but of endless development. There will always
be something new to achieve, learn or look forward
to; there will always be new songs of worship to be
written and performed. Matthew's life was not a
waste but a preparation for the full and unique
part he is now playing in the progress of heaven.

One of my favourite aunts is Aunty Ruth, a
retired schoolteacher. On our return to England,

she wrote to our Ruth a lovely letter of comfort. In it she said, as an explanation of why God had allowed him to die, 'God must have a very special job for Matthew to do for him.' One job I could visualise him doing would be helping to introduce others who died as children to the glories of heaven. It's a job he would enjoy and be good at. But that's speculation and doubtless I won't know what Matthew is doing in heaven until I join him there.

The Bible also suggests heaven to be a place where worship is vital, creative and whole-hearted—a far cry from what worship is like in many churches on earth. Matthew truly did love and enjoy worship, but only when it was full of life, rhythm and happiness. Drums and keyboard, flutes and fiddles were his idea of instruments. For someone like Matthew, for whom earthly worship could be exciting and fulfilling, the worship of heaven must be wonderful beyond description. I imagine that his growing skill on the piano will not be wasted and that he has got his hands on a bigger and louder drum-kit than the one he fancied on this earth. His worship of God will be ecstacy for him. What joy it will be for us to catch up with Matthew and his heavenly drum-kit! Naturally, a person not in love with God on earth would be bored at the thought of eternal worship of him in heaven, however up tempo the beat. But a stupendous experience awaits those who have already caught, however tentatively, the joy of true worship and delight in God.

But supremely it is God who will take the eye and ear in heaven. Heaven is where God is. Jesus spoke of heaven being a sort of great feast or party with God as the host (Matthew 22:1–14). In Revelation chapter 21, the New Jerusalem, the new dwelling place for man and God which we know as heaven, is characterised above all by a relationship:

> Now the dwelling of God is with men, and he will live with them.
> They will be his people, and God himself will be with them and be their God. He will wipe every tear from their eyes (Revelation 21:3, 4).

When we peer through heaven's open door into its marvellous realities, even while we search for our son, it is the Lord who holds our gaze. It will be so for ever, for our ultimate aim in going to heaven will not be to find our son, but to worship the Lord with our son at our side.

A few weeks after the funeral the vicarage was burgled. The patio doors were ruined and the house was a mess but as we looked round we realised that very little had actually been stolen: just a few items of jewellery. The most important was Ruth's gold cross and chain. The episode at least proved to us what we had long suspected— that we didn't have a lot worth stealing! Other houses in the parish were also burgled at about the same time and many people were far more upset than we were. I think this was because we had a different perspective after losing Matthew and thinking about heaven:

> Do not store up for yourselves treasures on earth, where moth and rust destroy, and where thieves break in and steal. But store up for yourselves treasures in heaven, where moth and rust do not

destroy, and where thieves do not break in and steal. For where your treasure is, there your heart will be also (Matthew 6:19–21).

Our real treasure was in heaven. Our earthly treasures were never recovered, except for Ruth's gold cross. This was discovered buried in nearby woods by a man with a metal detector. It seemed that we couldn't lose the cross—or the experience of suffering that it symbolised! We were glad to get Ruth's necklace back but we couldn't let the burglary worry us over-much. We were less worldly-minded; more aware that our citizenship was in heaven. We no longer felt properly at home in this world!

This world is not my home—I'm just a-passing through,
My treasures are laid up somewhere beyond the blue,
The Saviour beckons me from heaven's open door,
And I can't feel at home in this world any more.

8
Healing

Our first Sunday back in England was two days after the funeral. I had decided to take the church services as usual. Avoiding it to nurse my private pain would only have made church harder the following Sunday. It was our annual Gift Day. This year it was for two projects—one in India and one in Nepal—set up through our old friend Margaret Cranston. Ruth's back was not yet strong enough for church pews and so she stayed with friends while Christine came to church by herself. During the communion administration, the choir were singing, 'Be still and know that I am God.' Usually I filter out the singing to concentrate on the ministry but one line suddenly came through to me, and to Christine kneeling at the communion rail, with great power: 'I am the Lord who heals your pain.'

Afterwards, comparing notes, we both felt that those words, coming at the moment I gave Christine the communion bread, were especially for us; the Lord was telling us that he would heal our pain, through the cross.

Writing ten months after the accident, I can say that much of our pain has gone for good while some is still with us – though, we believe, being dealt with.

There were so many different aspects of our pain. There was the enveloping pain of knowing that Matthew was dead, and the remembered horror of the circumstances. There was the waking every morning and remembering, and the going to sleep every night with nothing else on our minds. There was the pain of guilt. This had been sorted out in Innsbruck but not completely removed, so we kept having to deal with fresh waves of it. There were also the situations of everyday living that reared up to hurt us. I had once enjoyed hillsides and woodlands; now I just shuddered at the sight of them. I was unsure about whether I would ever be able to go hill-walking again. Badly stung by nettles on the Mayrhofen hillside, I only had to see nettles now to bring the horror flooding back. We had always enjoyed family holidays; now mention of our own or other people's holidays brought pain. The four of us had enjoyed swimming together; now there was the pain (for me) of having to change alone. I had loved building model railways with Matthew; now the model railway was a pain trigger, as was the nearby Sheffield Wednesday football ground where we had enjoyed so many matches.

Having to adjust quantities for three, and no longer having to take account of Matthew's favourite things, made shopping painful for Christine. Early mornings were especially hard for her, too. She and Matthew had always been up

together long before Ruth and me. Now she was up
on her own. This was the time when she did most
of her crying, at first waking every morning at
around 5 a.m. and then at a more normal time. At
meals we were very aware of the missing place at
our rectangular dining-table and tried moving the
furniture around and using an oval table. Also,
there was a stab of pain every time we walked past
Matthew's bedroom door; every time it was hot and
sunny as it had been that day in Mayrhofen; and
every time we saw a boy a little older than
Matthew—because we would never know him at
that age.

　　　Whether at home or outside, in crowds or
countryside, pain stalked our waking moments. It
also haunted our dreams, in frequent nightmares.
But the song had said, 'I am the Lord who heals
your pain.' People often say, 'Time is a great
healer,' and, 'Only time heals.' The question was:
Would we have to wait over the years for time to
heal, or would the Lord heal our pain in his time?

We knew that God had created us with the
potential for being healed. But, though healing can
occur, it doesn't always. Emotional scars are often
taken to the grave; untreated emotional pain often
results in physical illness. Burying pain is not healing it and in that case time will only dull the senses
and hide the hurts. So how does healing occur?

　　　We believed that Jesus could heal us and
that we were to trust him, the wounded healer, to
do this in his own way. Without his healing, we
couldn't be the people we ought to be for him. We
needed to be able to minister to teenage boys, not
shrink away in pain from them. The beauty of

creation should not make us wince but fill us with
joy in our Creator. We could never be whole and
healthy human beings if areas of life and experience were to remain closed off to us. We needed to
be available for God in all circumstances.

As we talked these things through and
wondered what to expect of God, we turned to our
Bibles and found much reassurance:

> He heals the broken-hearted and binds up their
> wounds (Psalm 147:3).

> Blessed are those who mourn, for they will be com-
> forted (Matthew 5:4).

> He himself bore our sins in his body on the tree, so
> that we might die to sins and live for righteousness;
> by his wounds you have been healed (1 Peter 2:24).

Some who are in deep need use God like a
crutch—to be picked up and used in crisis but
discarded when they have learnt to walk alone
again. For some he is just a strength and comfort in
time of need. But we decided that our faith should
not merely be a help but the crucial factor—
making us face the pains and questions in order
that Christ could heal, in depth and permanently.

We saw this healing in terms of 'peace'—
Jesus' gift to his disciples in the Upper Room
before his arrest.

In the Bible, peace is not just absence of
disturbance; like the Jewish word *shalom*, it has a
great positive quality about it, and suggests wholeness and positive well-being in relations with God
and others, and within ourselves. Since it is God's
desire for all men to be at peace, we knew it was

right for wounded and hurting Christians to seek
the peace of God that passes all understanding. We
needed him to take away the life-limiting
secondary pains of bereavement while leaving us
with our central grief encased in his peace. Peace
was not an alternative to sadness: we could experience both, but the grief could be shot through with
God's peace.

Over the months we experienced God's
healing peace particularly through the cross,
through prayer and through facing up to pain in
Christ's strength.

'I keep coming back to the cross,' Christine
said to me once when we were talking about these
things. 'It's the reason we can be sure of Matthew's
place in heaven; it's the reason we can be sure of
our own forgiveness; and it's where Jesus starts his
healing work. He didn't just die to set us free from
sin but to have our wounds and hurts put to death
in him. He died to heal, as well as save.'

She turned to the prophet Isaiah:

> Surely he took up our infirmities and carried our
> sorrows, yet we considered him stricken by God,
> smitten by him, and afflicted. But he was pierced
> for our transgressions, he was crushed for our
> iniquities; the punishment that brought us peace
> was upon him, and by his wounds we are healed
> (Isaiah 53:4, 5).

It was no accident, we believed, that the
word of promise about our healing had come at the
moment when I had given Christine the
communion bread symbolising Christ's body
broken for her on the cross. Each time I have taken

communion since Matthew's death I have taken it as medicine to heal my pain; and sometimes I have physically felt the strength, the peace and the healing of God flowing into me.

Several times the same thing has happened when I have been praying with Christine or with a small group. And, in our own early morning prayers, we moved on from a simple prayer for survival to a prayer for healing throughout the day. Christine's early morning prayer and Bible study time was crucial for her healing. It was often necessary, in the early days, for her to hold on to God's promises in order to have the courage just to get out of bed and face the day, rather than shut herself away and hide.

During this time, God gave us a much greater ability to pray in tongues and I believe this kind of praying played its part in our healing, enabling our deep emotions to rise to God in prayer.

One day I prayed about my mental associations with nettles. That day they seemed to leap out at me everywhere I went and I got stung a couple of times! But by the end of the day I had a new set of associations and felt healed of the emotional pain they had been causing me.

Again and again we found that healing from the pains of ordinary living came not by avoiding but by facing the situations that hurt us; just as an injection of a safe amount of an illness can give immunity from the real thing. If painful places, conversations, memories, situations were avoided, their pain seemed to bury itself more deeply in us. But if they were faced and borne, they were 'exorcised' or made less painful for the future.

A few weeks after Matthew's funeral, we went to spend a therapeutic week with Margaret's parents, and our friends, Bob and Doris Cranston, in North Devon. On the Sunday afternoon, we drove out to Ilfracombe together to walk along the coastal path towards Lee Bay. This was the first time we had attempted a proper walk since the accident, and we had to steel ourselves to do it. Even the act of putting on our walking boots filled us with dread. The metal fasteners on Ruth's boots had been damaged in her fall, and we needed to mend them with a pair of pliers before she could wear them.

Unusually for them, Bob and Doris missed the way in Ilfracombe and we began our walk by climbing a steep zigzag path up the cliffside. It reminded us irresistibly of the path in Mayrhofen. We kept a close eye on Ruth while trying hard not to be over-protective or off-load our fears on to her. The path was crowded with holiday-makers and there was a baby in our party, carried on his dad's back. We realised afresh what a very ordinary path we had been on in Mayrhofen and what a freak Matthew's accident had been. The great triumph was actually to walk such a path and to know that it would be easier to do so in the future.

On the way down we bumped into two old friends from Fulwood, Peter and Gill Wright. They had just arrived in Ilfracombe for a holiday.

'Did you know about Peter's motor bike accident?' asked Gill. 'The doctors warned me he wouldn't live through the night. But the Lord kept him alive and here he is walking up this hill!' Peter then told us about a couple they had just met in their hotel. Their son had had a miraculous escape from another motor bike accident and they believed that God had spared him for his own good purposes.

We tried to make sense of all this in the car on the way back. Peter had lived, yet Matthew had died. The point seemed to be that our times are in God's hands. So we should not worry about the length of our lives but trust him. Suddenly, a sparrow flew into the car bonnet, and I saw it lying in the road through my mirror as we sped away. My mind went to the verse:

> Are not two sparrows sold for a penny? Yet not one of them will fall to the ground apart from the will of your Father (Matthew 10:29).

Even sparrows are under God's protection until their time comes. Death to Jesus was not the final thing it is to many; it was the pathway to heaven's open door.

When we got back to the house I looked up the next verses:

> Even the very hairs of your head are all numbered. So don't be afraid; you are worth more than many sparrows (Matthew 10:30–31).

So we understood that Matthew, even more than that sparrow, would not have fallen to the ground if this had been outside the will of his loving heavenly Father. We were not to worry or be afraid but to trust and obey:

> Look at the birds of the air; they do not sow or reap or store away in barns, and yet your heavenly

Father feeds them. Are you not much more valuable than they? Who of you by worrying can add a single hour to his life? (Matthew 6:26, 27).

And so we began more fully to accept and trust the sovereignty of God and to find his peace in our loss. Also, we began to look for good to come out of that loss. In this connection, a verse which was given to us several times about Matthew, by ministers who had been praying for us, was:

I tell you the truth, unless a grain of wheat falls to the ground and dies, it remains only a single seed. But if it dies, it produces many seeds (John 12:24).

One of our most heartfelt prayers was that God would show us the reality of that verse in the lives of people who would come to a new or renewed faith through Matthew's death. It would be some consolation to know that Matthew's death had sown the seed of eternal life in others. We were often disappointed at people's apparent lack of response, but there were exceptions and the brightest of these was Iain, Matthew's St John Ambulance leader. In a letter he later wrote, he told his own story, which I quote, with his permission:

About two months before Matthew's death I came across a book written by David Watson, called *Fear no Evil* (Hodder & Stoughton). It told the story of the last few months of his life as he came to terms as a Christian with his cancer. It was the first Christian book I'd read, and to this day I don't really know what made me read it. I had never taken more than a passing interest in things Christian.

The effect of it was that I went on to several other books by the same author. I started asking myself questions like, 'What is the purpose of life?' and, 'What happens after death?'—issues normally only discussed with close friends over a few pints of lager. I thought that if the story of Christ were untrue that was the end of it, but if there was the slightest chance that even a small part could be true, it had to be the most important thing in my life. The problem was, how could I find out?

I had known Matthew for about two years, and he had a great deal of ability, a likeable personality and a memorable cheeky grin. Through him I got to know his family well enough to be impressed by the quality of family life they seemed to have together. Two days before the accident we had been talking about Matthew at a St John planning meeting. As I drove past his house on the way home I found myself thinking, 'How would you react if something happened to end the family life you've admired at the Jacksons?'

When I was told that Matthew had been killed, I put the phone down and cried—cried for the first time over someone's death. I am a qualified nurse and have seen death in many guises, but never like this. Why Matthew of all people? I went to the church service that evening, even though church services had never done anything for me in the past other than make me cringe. But there was real emotion in the packed church, something I had never seen in a church before, and I was most impressed with Tim Gregory who spoke with real strength and compassion.

Like everyone else, I was shell-shocked for the next few days and could think of nothing else. I thought, 'If there is a God, then he's not much of a person to let this happen, especially to this family of all families.' I nearly concluded in my own mind that he didn't exist.

On the day of the funeral we got all the members of the division to attend in full uniform and give Matthew a guard of honour, and we got all the lads to sign a card. I added a note saying, 'If there is a God, then I wish I could find him and know him, because without him death seems so pointless.' I knew I must talk to Bob about the things that had been going round in my mind but didn't know how to. But about ten days later, he wrote to me suggesting a chat about my comment on the card.

We talked for about two hours and many of my questions were answered or deepened. I asked how we could be sure the stories of Jesus were any more true than those about Robin Hood. I knew that Jesus was the crux of all my questions, and that if the story of the resurrection was true this meant everything. Bob lent me a book about the evidence for the resurrection, and I became convinced of it as a fact. We talked again and I asked about the consequences of the resurrection. Bob replied, 'It means Jesus is still alive, that God is God. Why not say a prayer and ask him into your life?'

I thought I understood what this meant and was apprehensive. I sat quiet for about five minutes, toying with the question. A gut feeling came over me to say 'yes' and I was about to agree when I found myself saying, 'Can I use your toilet?' Perhaps the most important moment in my life and it was tripped up by a desire to pass water! I returned with an empty bladder and we prayed together. It was the first time I had really prayed, except for asking 'God' for nice weather or a win on the pools. This time I was asking Jesus to come into my life. What a change of request!

There were no fireworks or blinding flash; in fact, nothing. I went home wondering what was going to happen now and whether I had done the right thing. I woke the following morning with a most depressing feeling in my stomach and was afraid I'd done the wrong thing. But I remembered I'd said in that prayer that I would entrust my life to Jesus, and that I'd said to him, 'Yes, I do trust you now.' The feeling went in a flash and I never again questioned what I had done. There was too much evidence to say otherwise.

The following week Bob presented me with a Bible. On the inside front cover he quoted: 'But the truth is that Christ has been raised from death, as the guarantee that those who sleep in death will also be raised' (1 Corinthians 15:20–TEV). This is what I base my faith on, faith which is very young and has much to learn. I wonder what God has in store for me next?

There was great joy at the Confirmation Service a few months later when the Bishop of Sheffield returned to St Mark's for the first time since Matthew's funeral to confirm, among others, Iain and two of his St John Ambulance cadets. We were beginning to see our seed which had fallen to the ground, bearing fruit.

We were aware of the ways in which God was healing us, but it would be wrong to suggest that there were no ups and downs. Christine's daily Bible study and prayer-time which had sustained her for the first six months suddenly seemed to do so no longer. She needed deep reassurance that Matthew really was in heaven, and reasons for believing that Matthew's death was not utterly pointless, but her prayers along these lines did not seem to be answered. So she became angry with God, wondering if he really cared—and said to him: 'Just what do you expect of me? If you don't want to answer my prayers, suit yourself!' Eventually, realising that she was gripped by emotional rather than coherent doubts, she decided, as a pure act of faith and will, to accept that Matthew certainly was in heaven. After this, the problem retreated so suddenly that she felt as though it had been caused by a spiritual attack that had been repelled.

The teacher in Christine began to realise that, in not obviously answering prayers straight away, God was being a good teacher. Instead of making things easy for her, he was wanting her to work things out for herself.

As well as the Bible, there were other books which she found helpful, including John Wenham's *The Goodness of God** (IVP) and Tom Smail's *The Forgotten Father* (Hodder & Stoughton).

And so, in all kinds of ways, God's healing love and peace came into our lives as part of the continuing process of making us whole.

---

* Republished as *The Enigma of Evil*.

9
Difficult Days

If you ask a bereaved person, 'What are the worst times?' he or she will usually reply, 'Anniversaries and Christmas.' In the beginning, every Tuesday was a hurdle to overcome, and then it was every tenth of the month until about 4 p.m. when the worst had happened. Matthew would have been eleven on November 6th, nearly five months after his death, and we expected to shed some tears around that time.

Five days before Matthew's birthday, November 1st, was All Saints Day—the day on which the church on earth celebrates its fellowship with the church in heaven:

Come and see the shining hope that Christ's apostles saw;
On the earth, confusion, but in heaven an open door,
Where the living creatures praise the Lamb for evermore:
Love has the victory for ever!

Power and salvation all belong to God on high!
So the mighty multitudes of heaven make their cry,
Singing Alleluia! where the echoes never die:
Love has the victory for ever!

This festival had never meant much to Christine before, but this year she found she could remember Matthew with pride, and be thankful that he was still part with her of all Christians, living and departed. Thinking of Matthew's birthday in that context was a great help.

November 5th was the day we felt at our worst. During the afternoon Christine remembered vividly how she had been icing Matthew's cake a year before, and so the tears came. In the evening we went round to a church homegroup firework party and the rockets brought tears to my eyes as I remembered the long night eleven years earlier when Matthew had been born. But we were helped by the sensitivity of family and friends, and their gifts of flowers.

On Matthew's birthday, his gravestone was put into place. We had thought long and hard about the words on it:

Matthew William Jackson

Died 10th June 1986

Aged 10

A Gift of God

Much loved and missed

Now with his Saviour

It felt good to have the stone in place. Visiting his grave made Ruth and me feel a little closer to Matthew. By contrast Christine felt very little at the graveside. To her it seemed that Matthew was very definitely not there. He was 'now with his Saviour'. I agreed with her about that. A line from

a Christian song always echoed round in my head
as I arrived at the grave:

> *Why seek the living among the dead?*
> *Jesus is risen just like he said.*

So I knew that visiting the grave did not
really keep us in touch with the Matthew of the
present. He was in that mighty multitude singing
'Alleluia!' where the echoes never die. But it was,
for me, a way of staying in touch with the Matthew
I had known, and a place where tears—therapeutic
ones—could flow.

Another difficult anniversary was
Mothering Sunday. Christine drew comfort from
the fact that her task with Matthew had been
completed; that she had given him all that he'd
needed to make his way to heaven. But that didn't
make the day itself much easier to bear. The
previous year Matthew had brought Christine a
cup of tea in bed. This year obviously he couldn't
do that and there was only one bunch of daffodils
for mum in the church service.

Both Ruth and Christine cried a lot that day.
They both needed to draw on their reserves of
courage and faith in order to take part in the
morning service: Ruth read a lesson and Christine
helped her Boy Explorers to lead the prayers.

Christmas is the time when the emptiness
and longings of family bereavement are at their
sharpest. But for a vicarage family there was the
added pressure of extra work. There was a
crowded programme of events to fit in between
sermon preparation, visiting, and administration.
My part-time secretary had just left for a full-time

job and so I was coping with the office work by myself. I had no time either to dwell on having a Christmas without Matthew or to be in touch with my own feelings. When Christine asked me, 'How are you?' I had to reply, 'I don't know.' The bereft father in me had been driven underground by the busy vicar.

I made several attempts to get Christine a present, when I had a few minutes in town after a funeral at City Road or a visit to the printers. But I failed to find anything that seemed right, so I asked her to look out for something for herself. This proved too much for her.

'I'm not angry,' she told me, weeping. 'I'm just upset at coming bottom of the pile—you've always time for everyone else but me!' I responded by voicing my feelings: '*You're* not bottom of the pile, love! *I* am! I don't have time for my own feelings at all. I'm sorry about the present, I'm still hoping to get out again on Christmas Eve. But I desperately need your help to stop me getting to breaking point myself with all the pressure on me.' Christine understood, had compassion on my predicament and happily bought herself something on Christmas Eve.

We found that the general pressures of life in a vicarage were much harder to cope with when we had our own agenda of bereavement to work through at the same time.

But we did have one free evening together in the weeks before Christmas when we talked about Christmas past and Christmas present.

Suddenly, I experienced something that an old person would understand very well: a vivid sense of the past. It seemed as though time had telescoped; as though my young manhood, adolescence, and childhood were only moments away. I could feel myself a child again excitedly opening my Christmas presents!

I had talked with many old people and had discovered that the distant past was always vivid, real and immediate to them; their childhoods, though so long ago, were present to them. One of these old people was Christine's grandfather. We had visited him in the last weeks of his life when he had been ninety-six years old.

'It's a funny thing, memory. It's a funny thing, life,' he'd mused, as his eyes had gazed into the far distance and he'd fought again the battle of the Somme in 1916. His life had been long yet to him, looking back, it had all been over in a flash. Pondering on this, Christine and I reminded ourselves that with God a thousand years are as one day, and a day as a thousand years. Matthew's 'day' had lasted ten years; his great grandad's, ninety-six. But what difference did that make to God? How could either ten or ninety-six compare with eternity?

Also, it's the quality that counts. Martin Luther King knew this. Before his death, he made a speech about having been to the mountain top and seen the Promised Land. Therefore, he'd said, he was not afraid of death. Then he'd added a phrase which had always stuck in my mind: 'It's not how *long* you live, it's how *well* you live.' That, surely, I told Christine, was God's perspective on life and should be ours as well.

'In my better moments that's how I see it,'

she replied. I knew what she meant.

'We're only human, I'm troubled by the same doubts as you,' I replied. She responded, 'Yes, what if it's not true after all—everything we believe about God, and Jesus and heaven?' Then she added, 'Even if it weren't true, I'd still rather be a Christian than anything else. At worst our faith is just a helpful delusion which will die with us when we cease to exist.' She concluded, 'But we know it's not a delusion really. That's just a fear that comes to haunt us. We've too much experience of God to fall for that lie.'

We talked also, of practicalities. Ruth was adamant that the family part of Christmas should be just as it had been the previous year. However, we added a few extras, such as taking her out with us for an enjoyable pre-Christmas meal at a hotel.

Writing the cards was difficult, partly because it entailed Christine having to look again at the letters which we had received when Matthew had died, in order to find addresses. Other things, like the baking, she genuinely enjoyed at the time, and then had a good cry afterwards. The anticipated things were easier to cope with: we could pray and trust God about these in advance. But involuntary thoughts were harder to handle. While out shopping, Christine once found herself thinking, 'That would be a good present for Matthew to get his dad.' And on December 10th she suddenly remembered with a pang, 'Six months today!' Unexpected realisations like these caused surges of grief all over again.

Ruth had been chosen to be Angel Gabriel in the Nativity Service. We were very proud of her, not just because she played the part well and looked beautiful, but also because she seemed to be a shining example of God's healing at every level. We were buying her a bike for Christmas as she was now fit enough to ride one. Emotionally, too, she had made a good recovery and was down to earth and sensible about her grief, showing surprising maturity for an eight-year-old. She was able, for example, to enjoy putting up the Christmas decorations at home while talking about past years when she and Matthew had made some of the decorations for the tree themselves.

Christmas Day itself was not as difficult as we had thought, partly because Ruth so obviously enjoyed opening her presents and partly because the inner voices seemed to be strong again just as they had been in Innsbruck. Before we opened our presents early on Christmas morning, Christine walked into our laundry room and saw the flowers she had bought for Matthew's grave. She was lamenting that it didn't seem much to buy for him and remembering the high-speed diesel train we had bought him last year, when a voice said to her, 'What do you give to someone who really has everything?!'

On waking, my first thoughts had been along the lines of: Oh yes, Matthew's dead. Poor Matthew, missing out on Christmas Day. He would have loved it so much. Then his voice seemed to speak clearly in my head: 'It's Christmas every day here, Dad.' So I thought: 'It should be Matthew feeling sorry for us, not the other way round!'

Matthew's little cousin, Naomi, seemed to come to the same conclusion.

'It's Bob, Christine and Ruth's first Christmas without Matthew,' she said to her mother.

'Yes, but he's in heaven,' her mother replied.

'That's all right then, he's spending Christmas with Jesus,' was Naomi's response.

We found that our attitude to Christmas had changed because of Matthew. Christine voiced this thought when she said, 'Christmas helps me believe in the communion of saints more than anything.' She added, 'I know when Revelation describes the worship of heaven, it's all about Easter and the lamb who was slain for us. But it's all one story about God rescuing the world through Jesus. He began the rescue at Christmas. I don't understand all the philosophical questions but they've got to be celebrating Christmas in heaven. And I can feel close to Matthew celebrating it with me. That's why it's so important this year to celebrate the Christian Christmas, not the tinsel one.'

And so we felt much more deeply than before the hollowness of the standard British Christmas. We shrank from the superficial party-going and wept for all those for whom Christmas was nothing more than a traditional family celebration. By enjoying the good they had missed out on the best. Also, they were holding on to something essentially very fragile and temporary. We felt that Christmas for most people was a cruel sham. It always failed to deliver the goods. After the 'hype' of the adverts and the build-up to the holidays, the time itself was usually an anti-climax. The Christmas which had promised to be life-changing wasn't anything of the sort. It was a celebration, certainly, but most people didn't know what they were celebrating. The celebration had become an end itself: self-indulgence for its own sake. If for us Christmas had merely been a celebration time with the children, it would have been intolerable. We would have been one family among millions of others for whom Christmas spells emptiness and wistful longing.

Instead we could fill our Christmas with Christian worship and fellowship, and celebrate the heart of it with even greater depth than before. I had always hated the 'robin and snow-scene' style of card and we tried to send 'proper' Christian cards. This year very many of the cards we received seemed to be wishing us the peace of Christ. Perhaps the prayers behind our cards were having their effect.

I tried to express our thoughts in a Christmas sermon:

'Only Christians know what they are celebrating at Christmas. It's not food and drink, or holidays and parties. It's not even children. That would be to celebrate the good instead of the best. We celebrate Jesus Christ, the Son of God, born to save us and be our way to heaven. If our own family Christmas were centred on the children, where would we be this year? But I can still know peace and rejoicing at Christmas because for me it's centred on Jesus. There is nothing and nobody that can take Jesus away from me. A Christmas based on family tradition and the happiness of children is a fragile thing. Sooner or later it will let you down if you live long enough. But nothing and nobody can take a Christian Christmas away from you. Materialists can take a shallow pleasure in Christmas sometimes, but only Christians can rejoice in Christmas whatever the circumstances, whether they are on earth or in heaven, glad or grieving.'

Afterwards we sang:

> *Good Christian men, rejoice*
> *With heart and soul and voice;*
> *Now ye hear of endless bliss;*
> *Joy! Joy!*
> *Jesus Christ was born for this!*
> *He hath oped the heavenly door,*
> *And man is blessed for evermore,*
> *Christ was born for this!*
> *Christ was born for this!*

Not that things were easy. Wearing the vicar's smile and sharing the happiness of other families who were still complete was tough. But this Christmas we strongly sensed the reality of that door into heaven which Christ had opened. We knew with great clarity and simplicity what Christmas was really about, and this was exactly what we needed. Our whole life and existence, all we stood for and clung to, was riding on the truth of that carol. Without the truth it contained we would be destroyed; with it, our peace and joy that Christmas and for the years ahead were invincible.

> *Good Christian men, rejoice*
> *With heart and soul and voice;*
> *Now ye need not fear the grave;*
> *Peace! Peace!*
> *Jesus Christ was born to save!*
> *Calls you one and calls you all,*

To gain his everlasting hall.
Christ was born to save!
Christ was born to save!

10
To Calcutta with love

Wisps of snow curled in the biting east wind as I locked the church door at the end of the morning service. It was the second Sunday in January and Grenoside, seven hundred feet high on the eastern flank of the Pennines, felt like Siberia. It seemed that everyone in the congregation had clasped me by the hand and warmly wished me, 'Godspeed.'

'We'll pray for you while you're away. Come back safely, won't you?' they had said warmly. With an aching right hand but in good heart, I trudged back up the icy hill to 'Wuthering Heights', otherwise known as St Mark's Vicarage.

Later, after a last walk with Sam, the three of us drove down to Sheffield Station for the London train. Christine and Ruth bravely and energetically waved me goodbye from the platform as the train slipped out into the gathering blizzard.

My journey had had its origins in Matthew's funeral service. People had asked us if we would accept donations in memory of Matthew and we'd said, very willingly, that we would. When we'd been talking this over, Christine had said, 'I think we should send the money to Tear Fund because that was one of Matthew's own interests independent of us. So £1,300 (the amount donated) had been sent to Peter Jenkins. He'd forwarded this to Tear Fund Headquarters with an explanatory letter requesting that the money be used for a specific project. When Sally Lambert, the Overseas Family Care Director, had written back, suggesting that the money should go to a work among destitute boys in Calcutta, we'd been delighted. These boys had been previously fending for themselves on the great Howrah Station in Calcutta, but were now in a home called the Pauline Bhavan. They were all about Matthew's age and in great need, and railway stations had been Matthew's favourite places; so the idea had seemed particularly appropriate as a memorial to him. We had been especially moved by what George Hoffman (Tear Fund's Director) had written about the home, named after his wife Pauline (*bhavan* simply means 'home' in Hindi). Just outside the station he and his companion, Tony Neeves, had come across a boy lying in a gutter. This is how George described the incident and what happened next:

'He's dead, Sir,' said one of the porters.
'Been there four days,' commented another.
Sickened by the sight and stench Tony Neeves and I walked closer. He was a young boy who lay covered in filth and flies: a statistic—one of the 750,000 who live and die on the pavements of Calcutta—that took on flesh and blood reality. So, too, did the words of Rudyard Kipling:
Above this packed and pestilential town,

Death looked down.

Stooping down, Tony in a gesture of compassionate despair, waved away the flies that had settled on his eyelids and the insects in his mouth and nose. Then suddenly I saw his chest move.

'Tony,' I said, 'he's still alive.' Pushing through the crowds outside the most congested railway station in the world I found a policeman: 'There's a boy dying here in the gutter; he's been here four days.'

'Nothing I can do,' he replied. 'See my officer.' We did. He took our names and address and noted the incident on his pad.

'But he desperately needs help,' I explained as I pointed to the station gutter where he lay by Platform One.

'You can take him to hospital if you want,' he said. 'But no taxi will take you in case he dies on the way and they're held responsible. Try a rickshaw.'

We did. That posed another problem. The boy had now dragged himself painfully out of the gutter and lay spreadeagled across the pavement in a desperate attempt to shelter from the midday sun that now blazed down. The problem? Was he on the Calcutta side or the Howrah side of the station? There was a clearly defined demarcation between rickshaws and taxis that prevented this potential 'fare' being collected. By now we had worked through the emotions of sorrow and sympathy. And sadness. We were both angry. Very angry. We ran to find a friend's minibus. He threaded his way through the crowded streets and backed up to where the boy was lying. After he was carefully lifted on board, we drove him to Mother Teresa's nearby hospice where he was cared for.

As we drove on quietly, I realised afresh the

vital ministry that was being performed at our
destination—'Pauline Bhavan', a hostel called after
my wife, that has been established by Vijayan and
Premila Pavamani along with some other Christian
friends. It has been set up nearby Howrah Station
as a rescue and rehabilitation centre for some of
the 800 children and youngsters who have been
abandoned at the station. They live—and die, like
animals. They survive by committing every crime
in the book, under the control of gang-leaders that
make the Mafia pale into insignificance by com-
parison.

Inside Pauline Bhavan the contrast with the
world from which these children have been
rescued could not have been greater. Clean and
comfortable. Care and kindness. Love and
laughter. Prayer and faith. And hope.

At the moment there are just a few children
who have, literally, been rescued from hell. And it
started with just one. But that is what Tear Fund is
all about. No one person can change the world.
But I can help change the world for one person.
(From 'Tear Times' Summer 1986, by permission).

Each harvest the two churches and the two
schools in Grenoside combine to take gifts to the
local pensioners. This year we had already planned
to add a Third World project to our joint harvest
effort, so I had suggested raising more money for
Pauline Bhavan. Our Methodist friends and the
head-teachers had readily agreed to this. We had
decided on a sponsored swim so that Matthew's
friends could contribute by doing the swimming
and the whole community could join together in a
worthwhile project. Ruth and I had begun to train
together. The swimming was also part of Ruth's

physiotherapy and it was great to see her improving in her ability to swim longer distances.

The local swimming-baths had been booked for two consecutive Sunday afternoons and over a hundred of us, children and adults, had swum our lengths. Matthew's two best friends, James and Jonathan, with great determination had swum two miles together. Ruth and I had managed our half-mile each. As a result of everyone's efforts, we had been able to send off another £3,700 to Tear Fund, making £5,000 altogether.

The week of the swim, I had got a phone call from Philip Hacking, vicar of Fulwood.

'We would like to do something more in memory of Matthew over and above the memorial and sponsored swim money,' he'd said. 'We were talking about it at PCC last night and wondered if you would like to go to Calcutta to see the Pauline Bhavan. We'll pay the air fare. What do you think?'

'Oh Philip, that would be wonderful!' I had said.

So there I was on the London train travelling south through the blizzard.

I stayed overnight in Ashford with Matthew's godparents, Caroline and Ivor Houchen. After evening service, several old friends called round. There is still a close bond between Christian friends even after years of separation and we enjoyed a hilarious evening together. The next morning it was snowing, even in the Thames Valley, as Ivor drove me past the hospital where Matthew had been born, to Heathrow Airport.

The East begins at the Air India check-in

desk at Terminal 3. As we joined the milling throng, the monitor told us the news: our flight would be eight hours late—thanks, we later discovered, to fog in Delhi.

After a tedious day at Heathrow we were off. Russia looked dangerously cold from above. The white sheen of the deeply frozen countryside was reflected up in the light of the full moon. This was where Grenoside's east wind had come from.

Then we were over Samarkand and darker, warmer climes. Large curries were served in the small hours, high above the fighting in Afghanistan, followed by a dawn landing in Delhi.

Then it was a bus ride to Delhi's domestic airport and another all-day wait for my onward flight to Calcutta. I was beginning to feel that the conditions of modern air travel were a breach of the Geneva Convention, but late that night I arrived. I was met by the couple who were to be my hosts for the first two days in Calcutta—Wai and Rose Hu (pronounced Who).

'You're speaking at Calcutta Bible College at 9.30 in the morning,' said Wai as we drove into town in his Ambassador—a thinly disguised 1954 Morris Oxford and the commonest car on India's roads.

'What about?' I asked weakly.

'Whatever is on your heart. And then we're up at 5 a.m. the next morning to go to Jamshedpur, and you're preaching at Emmanuel Chapel, Sunday morning and Carey Baptist Church, Sunday evening.'

'At least I won't be bored!' I thought to myself as my head hit the pillow at the end of the forty-hour journey.

I was duly delivered to the Bible College in the morning. There I spoke about a Christian theology of heaven in the context of losing Matthew. My listeners were about fifty theological students—all training for ordination or missionary work. For some, English was only their third language, but they seemed to understand what I was saying; they even laughed at my jokes! The minister of Carey Baptist Church then gave me a conducted tour of his famous and historic church building, next door to the college and built by William Carey the pioneer missionary in India. Above the entrance was Carey's great motto: 'Attempt great things for God; expect great things of God.' I was to spend my week in Calcutta meeting Christians who were doing just that.

Wai took me next door to the building he and Rose used for their Feeding Programme financed by Tear Fund. About forty children—whom they have helped to put into English medium day-schools—came from the nearby slums to their centre each day, in order to eat a meal, have a decent sleep and do their homework. They sang Christian songs to me in Hindi and English. I told them about Matthew and stressed how important it was that, as well as doing their schoolwork, they should learn about Jesus when they were young.

After lunch we visited the tenement blocks where some of these children and their families live. Some had a room to live in, others lived in the doorways of other people's homes. In each tiny, overcrowded home I was asked to pray with the family. It seemed that the love of Christ was invading the tenements through the love Wai and Rose were showing for the children.

A million people live on the pavements of Calcutta. It is an easy city to weep over; the flood of human affliction engulfs the visitor. But visiting the families, sharing their hopes, problems and prayers, enabled me to enjoy the humanity of the individual rather than be lost in helpless pity for the plight of the anonymous masses.

We found Sunita, a teenager on the Feeding Programme, in bed in a hopelessly overcrowded tenement block. She had had a small operation the day before and did not as yet know the prognosis. But there was a radiance in her eyes as she talked of her hope of becoming a nurse, and a real trust in Jesus as she asked me to pray for her health. I went out rejoicing that I could visit some of the worst slums in the world and there meet Christ.

Not till we visited another family, where the father was ill in bed, did I realised that Wai, as well as being a 'Samaritan', was also a doctor. I was assaulted on the way out by a Hindu eunuch, dressed up as a prostitute and trying to make me give him money to get rid of him. But even that couldn't dim my amusement at being with a real live Doctor Who!

Wai then took me sightseeing and taught me that Calcutta is a city to be enjoyed. We took a ferry across the vast, ethereal Hooghly River to Howrah Station on the other side, where we joined the crowd on the little wooden landing stage awaiting the large overcrowded ferry now sliding sideways towards us.

'Isn't it going to be a bit overcrowded when they try to get off?' I asked, a little apprehensively.

'There's an understanding,' Wai replied. 'We all stand aside to let them get off first.' Just then it became apparent that the gang-plank would be some yards away from where we were standing.

'Can you climb railings?' shouted Wai as he leapt across the gap to the incoming boat, and proceeded to shin over the side. I could either follow or get lost in the crowd. I followed.

Howrah Station, where the Pauline Bhavan boys had once lived, begged and stolen, is the busiest in the world. The endless moving mass of humanity at its entrance was like an FA Cup Final crowd turning out of Wembley Stadium at the end of the game, except that here there was a second crowd trying to get in and the crush went on all day. We managed to find standing-room in a tram to take us back over the great Howrah Bridge to where we had left our Ambassador. But once over the bridge the tram went the wrong way for us.

'You can jump off trams, can't you?' shouted Wai as he fought his way to the exit and then leapt off the rumbling vehicle into the traffic. Feeling like a schoolboy back in Sheffield again, I shouted, 'Yes!' and followed.

The alarm call duly came at 4.50 next morning in time for the two of us to catch the 6.20 Ispat Express from Howrah to Tatanagar, four and a half hours due west of Calcutta. At Kharagpur Junction we alighted for a moment to admire the longest railway platform in the world and began to stroll up the platform in the morning sun.

'It's all right,' Wai reassured me. 'The train

always waits for quarter of an hour here.' Just then
the engine hooted and the train began to pull out.
We leapt on to the nearest coach and began walking back down the train to our reserved seats. But
the corridor connection was locked! As the train
picked up speed, we leapt off again and Wai
jumped into the next coach. No room for me there,
but I determinedly made it, running at top speed,
two coaches later. After all, Wai had the tickets.

We arrived safely at Tatanagar station, next
to the famous Tata Steelworks. A hectic twenty
minute auto-rickshaw ride through the city of
Jamshedpur brought us to our destination—Grace
Bible College. At the entrance to the small, half-
finished building we were greeted by the founder
and principal, Cyril Peters. Cyril had taught at
Calcutta Bible College before moving to pastor a
church in Jamshedpur. In 1982 he had felt that
God was calling him to found a small theological
college locally, teaching in Hindi to students who
would find the English medium difficult. He began
with no premises, students, staff or money and had
built the college up 'on faith'. I was reminded again
of Carey's slogan: Cyril was both attempting and
expecting great things. He took me to the roof of
the college and showed me the view out to the surrounding hills and villages. There were churches in
Jamshedpur but not in the villages. Cyril had had a
vision that one day his students would found
churches in them.

The college operated a Tear Fund Feeding
Programme similar to Wai and Rose's. Tear Fund
also provided finance for school fees, medical
expenses and clothing for the children on the

scheme. The poverty of the surrounding families
was obvious as we went visiting in the afternoon.
But when the children came after school they were
happy and healthy, ready for their main meal of
the day and a period of homework in the college
teaching room. The students helped to care for the
children as part of their practical training. It was a
joy to take photographs of them all before it was
time to find an auto-rickshaw and head back to the
station and the train to Calcutta.

That night I went to stay with Vijayan and
Premila Pavamani and their four beautiful
daughters in their Calcutta flat.

There, high above the horn-honking chaos
of Calcutta's traffic, Vijayan, eyes flashing and
arms whirling, told me the story of how Pauline
Bhavan had started. It was made the more vivid by
the fact that he had just picked up Premila whose
train had arrived late at Howrah Station because of
an accident: a boy had been seriously injured
through falling out of the train or, more likely,
being pushed out of the train by a man who'd
decided the boy was in his way. But after a while
the train moved on and on Premila arrived safely.

Vijayan said, 'I was at Howrah Station waiting for Premila. She was coming from Bombay and
the train was three hours late. Just like it was today!
In front of me a group surrounded a man and
started throttling him with a towel. When he was
helpless they kept punching him on the nose.
There was blood everywhere. Hundreds of people
could see it but they did nothing. They just passed
by on the other side.'

'I bet *you* didn't,' I thought to myself,

knowing that Vijayan had started the Samaritans in Calcutta.

'I don't know what happened to me,' he continued, 'but I went mad. I waded in, pushing the men aside and shouting. "What are you doing?" I must have put them off because I was able to lead the man away. I took him to a café and bought him a cup of coffee. I discovered he spoke my own language from the south—Malayalam. It spells the same backwards as forwards and it's the only language you'll need in heaven. I asked him what it was all about and he cried as he told me, so I knew he was genuine. He was part of a gang who queued for reserved seats on the trains and sold them to passengers on the platform at a profit. The point is, you can queue for hours for a reserved ticket here. His customer had taken the ticket and refused to pay more than the standard price. When the gang-leader asked him for the profit, he didn't have it and so he was accused of cheating. I gave him the money that was needed and he went to pay the gang-leaders off. Then I went back to the platform to continue waiting for Premila. There I saw a large group of station boys, sitting on the concourse eating. But one of them was sitting and crying because he had nothing to eat. I went to the gang-leader, a big lad with a limp, and asked him why one boy had no food. He said they were thieves and what they stole they shared. That boy had not brought him anything that day, so he was not being allowed to eat. I gave him some money and told him to get the boy some food.

'Then the first gang came back—they had been spying on me in the café—and started to beat me up. Fists, elbows, everything went in, but what hurt most was my pride. Somehow, by a miracle, I got away from them, but as I did so I caught sight of the boy whose food I had bought. And, oh, the look of helpless horror on his face as our eyes met! It was at that moment that I knew God wanted me to start a work with these boys.

'I mentioned the idea to Tear Fund. At first they said I had too much on to start another project: we were just setting up our Midway Home for drug addicts at the time. Then, after a year or so, they suddenly said, "We haven't forgotten your project for the station boys and have authorised the money if you can get the project going."

'The very next day I was riding in a car with a very well-to-do lady who told me about premises in Howrah. She said that a rich industrialist might be prepared to give them to us, perhaps for a work with local women.

'Without consulting anyone, I went straight round and said we would take the house. It was so obviously God's timing. We opened the place on August 14th, 1985—on the very day that official Government permission was finally granted. The boys came, and it was so beautiful, the way they have responded to the first love and security they had ever known.

'Of course we have our problems. The premises are pretty confined, and in a terrible area of Howrah. One of our two couples running the home had to leave recently when the wife became ill. We had built up the number of boys to seventeen and then six of them ran back to the station. We had been treating one for TB. Without treatment he soon died. We would like to find new premises outside Calcutta at Narendrapur where the Midway Home is. We looked all last year, but everything fell through. But we know that the Lord has given us this work and so we trust him for the future.'

I was very moved by the story, and said, 'God gave you the work and the vision—and he will cut through all the difficulties and give you the new vision at the right time.' A verse of Scripture— from the *Authorised Version*—came vividly to my mind. As I tried to remember the exact words, I realised that one of my hands was resting on a Bible which, to my delight, proved to be an *Authorised Version*. I looked up the verse and read it to my new friend:

For the vision is yet for an appointed time, but at the end it shall speak and not lie: though it tarry, wait for it; because it will surely come, it will not tarry (Habakkuk 2:3).

11
Pauline Bhavan

Seventeen of us set off in the minibus for Pauline Bhavan on the Saturday morning: twelve girls from Emmanuel School (which used the chapel building on weekdays); their dancing teacher; Vijayan and Premila; the driver and myself. We fought our way, through the snarling traffic, over the Howrah Bridge, past the station and into the back streets of Howrah—mean, dirty, dusty, narrow and hopelessly jammed with humanity, hand-carts, rickshaws, scooters, cars, buses and—above all—lorries. The combination of fumes and dust attacked my throat as the bedlam assailed my ears. It is possible to get stuck into a Howrah traffic jam all day, and this almost happened to us. Only expert driving and local knowledge got us through. But the girls were happy and excited, especially when we saw a train. They rarely left the slum district of Calcutta around Emmanuel Chapel. To cross the great bridge and see the great station was a memorable outing for them.

We stopped to buy oranges from a street-seller opposite a fish market.

'That old fish market burnt down one night recently,' said Premila. 'No one knows whether the fire was deliberate or not. Quite a lot of the station boys were sleeping there; they were killed—some of them were friends of our boys.'

We moved deeper into the Howrah nightmare and, eventually, in an area of ramshackle factories, we arrived at Pauline Bhavan.

The home was part of an old colonial house now mostly decayed. It felt like an oasis. The boys rushed out to greet us. There were eleven of them. I hugged each of them and we talked a little broken English together. I gave each boy a sticker—a colourful animal picture with the words 'God is love'—which was a present from Ruth. They sang some Christian songs for me in Hindi and then in English, including: *I stay right under the blood where the Devil can do me no harm*. Then the children had their dancing lesson while I toured the premises with the warden, Desmond Tully. A decision had recently been taken to retain the premises, perhaps as a half-way house, even if the new premises in Narendrapur should materialise; and some of the boys were busy whitewashing the kitchen and plastering a shed to convert it into a workshop.

I had brought with me from England about £120 for the home. Much of it had been collected by an Explorer Sunday School group at Fulwood. Their leader, Betty Underdown, had been both Matthew's schoolteacher and his Sunday School teacher. Every week since hearing about Matthew's memorial money, their collection had been saved for the Pauline Bhavan boys.

Desmond thanked me for the money and suggested that some of it might be used to make up into bicycles for sale. The rest, he thought, could be used as starting capital for a scheme to buy parts for making up strings of fairy lights to sell in the market. The idea is that, though starting capital may come from England, projects like Pauline Bhavan should become self-financing after a time. Also, the boys themselves needed to learn skills with which they could earn a living when they were grown up.

It was decided that the £5,000 from Matthew's funeral and the sponsored swim should be retained until needed to help purchase the new premises in Narendrapur.

The dancing over, I spoke to the boys, with Desmond translating, about my reason for coming. I told them about Matthew and his love for people like them, stemming from his love for Jesus. I explained how he had died and how the money had been raised. There were tears in the eyes of these tough but affectionate street urchins as I spoke. Then I presented them with the two large boxes of 'Lego' that had filled my suitcase from England—one a present from St Mark's, and the other from my sister Sue and family. The boys had never seen anything like it before but were soon playing with it happily. I stayed and joined in for a while and then it was time to go.

It was hard to say goodbye, and I would have loved to have taken one of the boys home with me to fill our depleted vicarage with the noise of his happiness. But this would not have been possible. So I had to say goodbye to Ratan from Bangladesh who had seen his father shot dead by border guards as they'd tried to cross into India. He had somehow found his way to Howrah station where he had existed by begging.

Another boy it was hard to leave was Bablu Das. Apparently abandoned by an aunt at the station, his earliest memory was of begging there. He had been taken on by a Fagin style gang-leader. But a taxi had run over his legs while Bablu slept one night. The other boys took him to the government hospital for treatment. When Vijayan found him the bandages and wounds were dirty and the stitches had not been removed. With care and treatment at Pauline Bhavan Bablu had recovered and was running around with the other boys. Also, he had responded to the love of Jesus expressed through the love of the Christians who had found him, and had made a Christian commitment. Wearing his sticker from Ruth, he proudly posed for my camera. The love of God had broken through the evil of man to become reality in the heart of a child of suffering. Here, where life was generally rated as unbelievably cheap, was living proof that the individual was precious to God and to his people.

A few weeks later, Bablu Das sent me a painting of the Howrah Bridge and a short note which he had been helped to put into good English:

Dear Uncle Bob,

Thank you for your visit to Pauline Bhavan. We really enjoyed that time with you. We thank God for the beautiful gifts you brought us. We are pray-

ing for you daily and pray that we also can show
Jesus' love to others like Matthew.

There was also a letter for Betty Underdown
from Shyamal, one of the other boys:

Dear Aunty Under Down,

Thank you so much for your gift and letter about
Matthew and your Sunday School. Because of your
love we have three bicycles and this has given us
much joy. We thank God for all the Sunday School
children and church members, especially your
personal concern. We are praying for you daily.

Next morning I preached at Emmanuel
Chapel, sharing with the congregation about
Matthew and my reason for being in Calcutta. I
had brought with me from England our St Mark's
Motto Card for 1987: 'Be joyful in hope, patient in
affliction, faithful in prayer' (Romans 12:12).

I also brought a visual aid in the form of
candles. The idea was that the candles represented
human happiness. I got some children to blow out
the first set of candles and said that, similarly,
ordinary human happiness could be blown out.
Then I asked them to blow out some trick party
candles. They didn't, of course, succeed. In the
same way, I said, true Christian joy can't be
extinguished even by terrible events. Though my
family's ordinary human happiness had been
blown out on that hill in Austria, our Christian joy
was shining more brightly than ever. I assured
them that it could be the same for them in their
precarious situations in Calcutta.

That afternoon we drove out in Vijayan's

Ambassador to the Midway rehabilitation home for drug addicts. It was a difficult hour's drive to the edge of Calcutta, which Vijayan managed in forty-five minutes. I sat in the passenger seat, closing my eyes when I couldn't face what was going on.

'It was amazing how the Lord gave us this place,' Vijayan said. 'We'd been looking at a number of properties. As soon as we saw this one, I blurted out to the man who was selling it, "This is the place the Lord wants me to have." It usually spells disaster in India to let the seller know you really want what he has for sale, so I held my breath as I asked him the price, knowing that the house was worth at least ten lakhs—that's a million rupees.

'"Three and a half lakhs," was his reply. I was amazed. Tear Fund had authorised me to spend up to three. I asked, "Can I have it for three lakhs?"

'"Yes," said the man and I nearly collapsed. At the opening ceremony Mother Teresa was our chief guest—she sends me all her drug addicts now. The man who had sold us the property was a Hindu doctor, and he got up and made a speech: "I built this house for myself and my family to live in ten years ago. While it was still being constructed we had a visit from a Pundit (a Hindu holy man) who told me, 'You will not stay in this house all your life. It will go for an honourable work for God.' He was right, and this is the work."

'That put the seal on it; we knew this was God's work. There are about 100,000 drug addicts in Calcutta on a whole range of drugs. We have received about 600 so far at Midway. You saw some of them at church this morning. They've been cured and become Christians. It's beautiful.'

Much of Vijayan's time was spent seeing a constant stream of addicts and their parents at his office, and I knew he was very well known in India for this work, so my sense of anticipation grew as we approached the home. It was a beautiful villa with a green and shaded garden watered every day from its own pond. We were greeted by the warden, Mr Hartnett, an Englishman, with many years' service in the Indian Army. He had taken Indian citizenship.

'When I retired I decided it was time to do something for God,' he explained. 'The therapy includes daily Bible study and prayer and it seems to work.'

It was also a beautifully therapeutic place to be and I could understand why Vijayan had a vision of the two sorts of work in the same locality—Pauline Bhavan and the Midway Home.

'There could be a connection between them,' he explained. 'Apart from the fact that we could drive out to see them both at the same time, the addicts could help with the Pauline Bhavan work. They need useful things to do.'

I took a photograph of the plaque recording the thanks of the people of Calcutta to Tear Fund for the Home. Then, all too soon, it was time to return to the city.

Everyone was certain that Carey Baptist Church started its evening service at 6.30 p.m., and we just had time, driving at Vijayan's speed, to make it—or so we thought. But when I arrived, the service was well under way, having started at 6 p.m.

No one seemed perturbed that the visiting preacher had arrived so late, however, and I was quickly up into Carey's pulpit to preach. My text was:

> For God so loved the world that he gave his one and only Son, that whoever believes in him shall not perish but have eternal life (John 3:16).

This very well-known verse must have been preached on many times in that church over the centuries but perhaps my angle was different. I explained about Matthew and about how I had felt on the day my only son had been taken away from me. Yet God had willingly given his Son—that was how much he loved us. It was costly giving, I said, even though God had known that Jesus would rise from the dead. I also knew that Matthew was alive in heaven, but my grief was just as real. It was a staggering thought that the eternal God had willingly suffered and grieved for his only Son.

I told them about how Christine had become a Christian through looking at a picture of the cross and having a vision of Christ together with a vivid awareness of the depth of love that would go to the cross for her. She had realised that, even if she had been the only person in the world who had ever needed forgiveness, Christ would still have died for her.

As it was Missionary Sunday at Carey, I ended by challenging the congregation to respond with sacrifice to the love God had shown for them. I knew they supported a missionary from their church who was working in the Indian-owned Andaman Islands.

A long line of young Indians and Chinese shook my hand at the door on the way out. The Chinese, like Wai Hu, were from Calcutta's Chinatown just down the road from Carey. At the end of the line was a European—grizzled, elderly and very small. He wore an ancient dark suit, a soiled shirt, and a ramrod straight Sunday tie. As he spoke I realised why he had seemed so familiar to me. His demeanour and style of dress reminded me of the old Welsh gentlemen we used to see shuffling to chapel around Llanberis, clutching their black Bibles. His accent was pure, soft North Wales and his name was Roland Williams from Pant Glas near Llanberis.

'I was a farmer,' he told me. 'One day when I was working in the fields I had a vision of Christ on the cross dying for me. And I knew that he wanted me to go and work for him. I've been in Calcutta over twenty years, mainly distributing tracts in the slums but also prison-visiting and befriending the few Jews that remain here. People have suggested that I retire but I won't. I want to die serving the Lord in this place.'

Mr Williams was a very ordinary Welshman with a very simple lifestyle and hardly any financial support or needs. He was supported by no missionary society, for the one with which he had trained had turned him down for overseas work in 1949 on the grounds that he was too old! He was small and unassuming—an insignificant figure among the crowds of Calcutta. But he had held on to his calling from the green hills of Wales to the slums of India for thirty-seven years.

This humble, unknown man brought tears

to my eyes, as I grasped the magnitude of the quiet sacrifice of his life in response to the cross of Christ.

He still corresponded with his eighty-three year old sister in Pant Glas and so I promised to visit her for him next time we were in the area.

Next morning, Vijayan took me to visit Mother Teresa. Their Christian traditions were very different from each other, but they were close allies in the business of bringing God's love to the streets of Calcutta. Vijayan sent 'Mother' his destitute and dying, and she sent him her drug addicts. We arrived to find that Mother Teresa was out—on a business trip to Delhi. Vijayan was apologetic.

'Never mind,' I said. 'I expect her deputy is quite nice too!' And so she was. As we wandered through the main house with her, we talked of the nine and a half years of preparation before the sisters could become full members of the order. The aim in these years was to make them totally dependent on God and free of all worldly encumbrances. There were three hundred nuns living in this great house—surely the largest convent in the world.

We prayed in the simple but peaceful chapel as the blare of the traffic penetrated the windows to remind us of where we were. The stations of the cross along the chapel's back wall brought back vividly the path in Austria, and I marvelled at where my way of the cross had been leading me so far. I was meeting some wonderful people on my trip and every moment in India was filled with vivid events and stimuli. But I was on my own, separated from Christine and Ruth, and therefore feeling the loss of Matthew even more keenly. The days when we had been a complete, secure family before the accident, seemed so long ago and far away. Yet the presence of God and the love of Christians were all around me in this strange and extraordinary city. And, remembering the words of Paul, I knew that my real security could never be taken away from me:

> For I am convinced that neither death nor life, neither angels nor demons, neither the present nor the future, nor any powers, neither height nor depth, nor anything else in all creation, will be able to separate us from the love of God that is in Christ Jesus our Lord (Romans 8:38–39).

I also knew that, though separated from my family, I was nowhere separated from God—least of all in this chapel where his love seemed to have soaked into the walls. I remembered some verses of my favourite psalm:

> Where can I go from your Spirit? Where can I flee from your presence? If I go up to the heavens, you are there; if I make my bed in the depths, you are there. If I rise on the wings of the dawn, if I settle on the far side of the sea, even there your hand will guide me, your right hand will hold me fast (Psalm 139:7–10).

Time was short as I had a plane to catch later that day, and all too soon we left for Mother Teresa's Feeding Programme half a mile down the road. This was doing brisk business, mainly with destitute adults. And then we drove in the faithful Ambassador to the Mother's Home for the

Destitute and Dying. This was in a tough district and Vijayan first had to hire a man to watch the car before we could slip in through the unassuming entrance.

The place was smaller than I had expected, but full of people. There was a large number of sisters and foreign volunteers engaged in loving and caring. The atmosphere of the building reflected those qualities.

Vijayan introduced me to the sister in charge with the words, 'Meet the driving force.' She greeted us, all serenity and smiles. We talked of the contrast between being able to die with a sense of dignity and worth in a place of security and compassion, and dying in the gutter. We did a tour of the 'wards' and then Vijayan took me outside to show me the architecture. The building had clearly once been a Hindu temple.

'The Mother bought it from the man who owned the temple years ago,' he explained. 'Come round the other side. It's the most incredible contrast.'

He led me round the corner of the building along a side alley. As we walked past the stalls of traders in souvenir trinkets and flower garlands, he explained animatedly, 'This side is still temple. You can feel the atmosphere of the Home fading and then you can feel the evil rising in the air as you walk.' He was right! I could!

'You'd better claim the protection of the blood of Christ now,' he whispered as we picked our way through the crowd. I did, praying silently. He continued, 'It's a temple to the Goddess Kali. She is very powerful, but she only likes blood. She grants human desires for marriage, success in business and so on. But only for people who offer her blood. They used to sacrifice people once, but now it's goats and lambs.'

As we watched in the temple courtyard, a priest cut off the head of a goat and carried the carcass away—its legs still kicking in protest. The man to whom the animal had belonged dipped his finger in its blood and smeared this on his forehead.

'They identify with the slaughtered animal,' whispered my guide. 'They feel their sins are forgiven because they have bought the goat and its blood pays for their own sins.'

'You mean like the atonement sacrifices in the Old Testament?'

'Absolutely—they even have the tables of the temple traders that Jesus overturned in the Jerusalem Temple.'

It seemed to me that, as well as the temple traders, the owners of the temple must have been making quite a good living on the proceeds of the goats they sold. The clients were often educated and well to do. I supposed that was inevitable because the ordinary poor people could not afford the goats. Cleansing and forgiveness from Kali had to be bought, first with money then with blood, and the bigger the price the better the cleansing. That seemed to me to be the source of the smell of evil from the Temple side of the building. It was such a contrast with the other side where acceptance and forgiveness were freely given. There, God had given the blood of his own Son for cleansing, and demanded no other.

As we walked round to the other side again the feeling of oppression lifted and the atmosphere of love could again be felt—seeping out through the walls of the Mother's Home.

'The last visitor I took here was a chap called John John,' remarked Vijayan.

'Oh yes, I know him,' I replied. 'Matthew knew him as well and wanted him to come to Sheffield to do a mission at his own team's football ground.'

'Yes,' said Vijayan, grinning. 'When he saw the sacrifices, he fainted!'

We got stuck in the traffic on the way back. A political demonstration was blocking our route. We talked about Vijayan's future plans and projects—some of which were scheduled to receive help from Tear Fund.

'We haven't got the resources of Mother Teresa,' he said. 'She's a great businesswoman. I don't mean that as a criticism—all the best saints have to be practical. But we can't think glossy-big. Small scale, practical projects to show the love of Christ are what we look for. I want to do something for stranded ladies who come to Calcutta looking for work and run into difficulties before they can find it. What's needed is a small hostel to provide temporary shelter and security until they can support themselves without resorting to prostitution. Then there are the shoeshine boys. We'd like to set up ten boys with the proper equipment and help them with some management and pastoral support. The rickshaw wallahs—the ones who still walk, not the bicycle ones—usually have no shoes. In summer the roads melt in the heat and they have to walk barefoot on the tar. We want to provide them with sandals, and then perhaps help them form a co-operative with capital for buying new rickshaws. Then there are a million un- employed people in Calcutta. Where do you start? We want to start with some teenage boys who are already Christians. Give them a workshop, a manager, some tooling and marketing and give them a chance.'

As we sat, frustrated and fuming in the noisy jam, the overwhelming scale of all Calcutta's problems was borne in on us.

'You've got the right idea,' I said. 'One church can't change Calcutta. But it can change Calcutta for a few people. That's better than despair and private piety. It's the Christians who are making the individual precious in this city; it's the Christians who are showing what love is.'

With the help of heroic horn work and some daring U-turns, Vijayan fought his way back home to pick up my bags for the trip to the airport.

My pilgrimage to Calcutta was over. I had forged a bond with the boys who would be a living memorial to Matthew. But there was also a bond with many other people as well, and with the city itself. I would be back.

12
Mountains again

The plane left at dusk for Kathmandu. I had arranged to spend a week in Nepal with our missionary friend, Margaret Cranston, with whose parents we had spent a week not long after Matthew's death. She met me at the airport and we took a taxi to the headquarters of the United Mission to Nepal (UMN)—a consortium of missionary societies including Margaret's own, the Church Missionary Society. UMN is involved in education, health, and economic development projects in Nepal, working in co-operation with the Government. Some of the money raised at St Mark's annual Gift Day, the Sunday after Matthew's funeral, had gone to UMN for their college in Jumla, a remote town in Western Nepal. It had helped to finance the building of a hostel for students on a Health workers' training course. Margaret, a teacher, had just transferred from a village school in the hills to a boarding school in Pokhara, Nepal's second city.

Although the Government in Nepal

welcomes the development help given by UMN, it insists that it is against the law for people to change—or to persuade others to change—their religion. Missionaries, therefore, have to behave very carefully and only give an account of their faith if asked for one. Local Nepali clergy run a considerable risk, particularly when they baptise people.

We spent a day sightseeing in Kathmandu, looking at its many and varied Hindu temples. The next morning we set off for the hills.

There were ninety of us on the little coach for the seven-hour journey through the immense hills of Nepal to Gorkha—the town which gave its name to the famous British regiment. We stretched our legs by climbing up to a prosperous temple, two thousand stone steps above the town. At tea-time our porter arrived, barefoot, from the hills—ready for an early start next day. We went to our hotel and ordered chicken for dinner. Fast food took on a whole new meaning for me as the hotel staff went out to catch a bird scurrying around outside! As we waited for the meal to be cooked, we sat and talked in the candle-light.

We spoke of the resurrection hope that sustains Christians in bereavement and contrasted it with Hinduism.

'The Hindus don't really have a resurrection hope,' said Margaret. 'The best they can expect is reincarnation into a higher caste or, for the women, reincarnation as a man. The whole system is designed to keep people in their place. I was walking with a friend back to our village one Easter Sunday after visiting some other Christians. It was getting dark, and a lady joined in with us to avoid walking on her own. She seemed very despondent and began telling us her life story.

'"I was married from my mother's breast, that is, when I was three, and my husband died eight years later," she said. "I've been a widow ever since and now I'm over forty. In my culture among the higher castes it's a sin to re-marry. But it's also a sin to die childless. So I'm trapped between two sins and I must live and die in sin. There is no hope for me, is there?"

'"Yes there is," we said. "Our God can forgive every sin. It's Easter Sunday. We've just been celebrating Jesus' resurrection and his power to take away our sins. Jesus gives us eternal life, not reincarnation. That gives hope to us all."

'"But our priests never told us about this Lord Jesus who is willing to forgive and erase our sins!" she exclaimed in amazement. "Why have I lived in fear all my life? Why has no-one ever told me this before? Why have I lived all this time without hope? What must I do to make sure I have this life? I can't read or write and I might never meet another Christian."

'"You don't have to do anything," we said. "You can't earn eternal hope. It's given you by Jesus. Just accept his forgiveness and his new eternal life." Then our ways parted and we've never seen her since. We know of a young man from her village who has become a Christian and we just pray that they will meet up.'

The hen duly arrived on the table, and all its various bits were much enjoyed.

We left at dawn the following morning, with

our porter, for the walk to the village where we would stay the next night. The high, white Himalayas formed a spectacular backdrop to our magnificent walk over the steep, high hills of central Nepal. Once our path went through a school playground. The rare white faces were spotted and out came the schoolchildren and teachers to stare at us. I took some photographs and promised to send them copies. It was the only way that school would ever have a school photograph!

By afternoon we had reached our destination and were greeted by Chandy, a UMN teacher at the local school. He, like Vijayan, had originated from Kerala state in South India, but had emigrated to Canada where he'd found success as an oil company executive.

'We had everything—all the gadgets,' he said. 'We could change the car every year or two for a new one. But I thought, "Why are we doing this? We're just trying to keep up with everyone else. What's the point? We're not doing anyone much good." So we gave it all up and came here. We've got nothing any more but we're happy.'

'Yes, one of the happiest looking men I've ever met,' I thought to myself. Chandy was always making little jokes and laughing—and when he had no special reason to laugh, he just laughed anyway. The man who had given up the rat-race to serve God on a hill in Nepal was a man with a permanent grin.

In the evening Chandy's landlord arrived to chat and to view the visitors. He was well known in the village as a healer of sick children by the saying of incantations, and was one of its richer inhabitants. But he was not known as a contented man, and in truth had been more or less drunk all day. It was explained to him that I was a 'guru' visiting from England and so he decided I was the 'Great High Priest of England'—number one in our caste system pecking order. He offered me anything I wanted, even a cow. I declined the cow on the grounds that I was not sure what I would do with it!

Another dawn start began our next day's walk to the village where Margaret had previously taught. There would be a reunion for her at the end of the trip, and I had my own special purpose for it. That day there was no porter, so I plodded on more slowly—carrying my heavy rucksack and feeling the growing heat of the morning sun.

The country was magnificent and the mountains stunning. After Matthew had died, I'd wondered whether I would ever be able to go out for a walk again, even in our local woods. That hurdle overcome, I'd then wondered if I'd ever be able to go walking in the hills again. This, too, I had managed, by climbing Snowdon the previous summer. And now here I was in the Himalayas—tackling and so being helped to overcome my fear of wooded slopes not unlike those of Mayrhofen; added to this my pleasure at the beauty and grandeur of God's creation in that marvellous land soon overrode every other emotion. Now, I felt, there would no longer be any 'no-go' areas for me in God's world.

'Real hope takes away the fear of death for Christians,' commented Margaret, remembering the conversation of the previous night. 'One day I was walking up this path to school when I saw a piece of broken plough and a lot of blood. The children were giving it a wide berth and spitting in its direction. I walked straight past close by. At school I asked the other teachers what it was all about.

'"There's a man in the village whose daughter has typhoid," they replied. "He did the sacrifice in the night hoping the spirit of the typhoid would leave his daughter and enter someone who walked too close to the sacrifice."

'"Does that mean I'm going to get typhoid?" I asked.

'"Oh no," they replied. "It can't affect you because you're not afraid of it."

'You see,' Margaret finished, 'they live their lives in fear of the gods: there is no concept of a God of love.'

We breasted the last hill at noon and there below us was Margaret's old school. The classes were spread out in circles on the grass around the buildings. A figure who looked like a caretaker was going about his chores.

'That's Krishna,' said Margaret. 'His father died in debt, which he had to pay off, so he's very poor. He works all day at the school and farms some land at the bottom of the hill. He only gets £9 a month from the school so he needs the land to make ends meet. He used to be my landlord when I was teaching here. About three years ago his daughter Shanti—whom Krishna doted on—died suddenly one morning. No one knows why. She was about five. The neighbours told his wife that they must have done something to displease the gods—perhaps not making enough sacrifices—and so the gods had punished them. Three months later Krishna came to us and said, "When my daughter died, I realised our religion offered no hope and had nothing to offer me. So I decided I was going to follow the one true living God which you worship. Since then I haven't done any *puja*" (Hindu worship and sacrifice). "I've thrown out all our household gods and idols. They have no power to help or hurt us."

'This wasn't just a sudden impulse, for Krishna was an intelligent and thoughtful man, as Jean, the other UMN teacher at the school, explained to me: "One day, walking home from school, before Shanti's death, Krishna said to me, 'Miss, I don't think that these idols can really be gods at all!'

"I questioned him. 'What do you mean?'

"'He had never read the Psalms or Isaiah, where almost identical things are said, but he replied, 'Well, it stands to reason that they can't be gods. Just look at them—they have eyes, but they can't see; they have ears, but they can't hear us; they have mouths, but they can't speak to us; they have hands and feet but they can't walk or do anything! Besides that, they are made out of stone or wood. A man takes a chisel and he cuts out the idol—he makes it with his own hands and then he worships it! If a man can make an idol with his own hands, he must be greater than the idol. There must be something in the spirit of a man that causes him to make the idol; God must have something to do with the spirit of man and not with wood and stone.'

"'I was amazed at this speech," Jean went on, "but I had no chance to follow it up before Shanti died. I loved her almost like my own daughter and was shattered by the news. I don't know how I got through the first day when I heard. I went over to their house with some vague idea of bringing comfort; and all I could do was sit and cry with them. In fact I needed comfort myself because I had loved little Shanti so much. All I could do was to cry out to God in anger, despair and confusion, and my plaintive 'Why?' just bounced off the ceiling. I got my Bible and shouted out to God some of the Psalms that cry out to him in hurt. Then God seemed to tell me to pray those Psalms on behalf of Krishna and his wife, because they didn't know them. The next day I managed to give Krishna a copy of John's gospel in Nepali, with the passages about our hope of eternal life all marked. It was after he had read John's gospel that Krishna told us he wanted to be a Christian."

'A few weeks after that,' Margaret explained, 'we went and asked Krishna's wife, "What do you think about the new religion your husband has decided to follow?"

"'It's much better than the old one," she replied. We asked, "Don't you get trouble from your relatives?" She replied, "Yes, but I never knew my mother. She was my father's eighth wife. He kept marrying more to get a son. When I was born, my mother was so afraid of his anger at another daughter that she ran off. I was brought up by one of the other wives. Now I'm married and in a separate household, so I go with my husband.

We're in this together. We're bringing our two sons up as Christians."'

We walked down to the school and greeted the staff and pupils, taking photographs of them. I was particularly looking for certain boys, the poorest in the area. These would be wearing Matthew's clothes which the previous summer Christine had washed, ironed and sent out to Margaret to be given to the poorest of her school-children. It didn't take me long to spot the boys—including Krishna's son—who were wearing Matthew's shirts, jerseys or shorts. It was an emotional moment but also a highlight of my trip. The clothes were all grubby and worn because these kids had no others. But, clearly, they were needed and appreciated. Far better to have them used like this than to keep them in a drawer at home.

I explained to the head-teacher and to Krishna about Matthew and why these clothes from England had suddenly appeared. This seemed to make a bond between us. Child mortality is very high in Nepal and I was able to share in their experience.

All too soon it was time to leave, so we climbed down the great hill to the road and took the bus to Pokhara.

With the help of some aggressive pushing we were able to join a hundred others on the little bus for the four-hour run. For those under about five feet three inches, standing was not so bad. But for those, like myself, a little taller, head-room was as great a problem as foot-room!

Next morning we were mounting bicycles at

7 a.m. for the six-mile climb up the lower slopes of
Annapurna for church at 8 a.m. The service, at
which we sat cross-legged on the floor, lasted for
two hours and was in Nepali, so I found it hard to
join in, except when the hymn tunes also had
English words. The real pleasure lay in seeing the
joy and enthusiasm of some of the local Christians.
It certainly didn't matter that, Sunday being a
normal working day in Nepal, church was
happening on Saturday. It was just good to know
that all over the world it's possible to find fellowships of worshipping Christians.

We later visited a Tibetan refugee camp,
and saw the Tibetan traders arriving with their
horses from China. I was told that there is now a
Tibetan-speaking church in Nepal.

I hadn't thought it would be possible to find
a town with surrounding mountains closer or
higher than those round Innsbruck. But I had
been wrong. Pokhara fitted the bill. Margaret's new
school there was dominated by the towering un-
climbed peak of Machapuchare—the nearest of the
Annapurna range and, at twenty three thousand
feet, the lowest. Thanks to my time in the
Himalayas and at Pokhara, I would now have
memories other than those of Matthew's death to
associate with steep slopes.

After two contented days it was time to catch
the bus back to Kathmandu. The next day I took
the plane to Delhi. There, for two short nights, I
stayed with Premila's sister and husband—Helen
and Frank Suttle—who had booked me on the Taj
express to Agra.

The Taj Mahal had been completed by the

Mogul Emperor, Shah Jehan, in 1653 as a tomb and memorial for his lamented favourite wife. It was wonderfully beautiful, perfect in form and texture. But it struck me also as formal and cold—a sad extravagance by a Muslim whose concept of glory had been earthbound. Speaking of heaven, Jesus had said, 'In my Father's house are many mansions.' But Jehan had tried to build his heavenly mansion on earth. Perhaps that's why I found the place—skilfully constructed though it was—rather pathetic. And the Shah's story had had a sad ending, too. He had been desposed by his son and imprisoned in a room in Agra Fort overlooking his monument. There he had died.

Industrial pollution is now eroding the marble and the Taj Mahal may not survive intact much longer. How thankful I was that Matthew's mansion was eternally secure in heaven, and that our Indian memorial to him was not in marble that would crumble but in lives that were made for eternity!

It really was foggy in Delhi when the plane I was due to fly back on landed at the airport: it took the search vehicles thirty-five minutes to find it on the runway. But only three hours late, I took off for Heathrow. Flying up the Red Sea, with the green of the Nile in Egypt on the left and the barrenness of the Wilderness of Sinai on the right, I thought, 'No wonder the Israelites complained to Moses that things had been better in Egypt and asked, "Why did you not leave us in Egypt where the grass was green?"'

But, I reflected, God had been able to see further than the Israelites. His great purpose had been to lead them to the Promised Land and that meant going through the wilderness.

That set me thinking about the wilderness of bereavement which our family was going through. It was tempting for us to complain that things had been much better in our 'Egypt'—the time before Matthew's death. But God was leading us through the wilderness into our Promised Land which as yet only he could see. So I prayed that we would go on trusting him to do that.

Christine and Ruth met me at Heathrow. We had missed each other terribly because we needed each other so much. It was marvellous to be back together again and to look forward once more to God's future for our family.

13
Questions

It was late autumn, six months after Matthew's death, and I had just left for church one Sunday teatime. Christine and Ruth were sitting at the table in the kitchen.

'Mum,' said Ruth, 'if God loves us, why did he let Matthew die?'

Christine hesitated a moment, praying inwardly for some inspiration.

'God must have had a very big reason to let Matthew die,' she began. Then the inspiration came and she asked, 'Do you think that God loved Jesus?' Ruth's answer came quickly, 'Yes, of course.' The second question was, 'And what happened to Jesus?' Back came the reply, 'He died on the cross.' Christine said, 'God had a very big reason for allowing Jesus to die even though he loved him. Jesus died in our place and it was through Jesus that God was going to save the world. The reason why God allowed Matthew's death was not as big and important as that, but it was still very important for God to allow it to happen. Just as God loved Jesus and his family so he loves Matthew and us.' Ruth and Christine talked a little about what the big reason might be, chatting about our sponsored swim and the changes in some people's lives; and then Ruth, satisfied for the moment, ran off to play.

Ruth was voicing the question with which we had been battling: the universal question which bereaved people address to God. For those without a belief in God 'Why?' is really an expression of despair. They can find no sense or justice in what has happened, so their question can only be answered in terms of events which caused the tragedy.

Others believe in God but have no relationship with him through Jesus. For them, the question is often an angry one: 'Why have you done this to us, you wicked God?' They had thought of God as the one who protects decent people like themselves. Now they are disillusioned.

A better answer to the question of suffering runs something like this: Jesus never promised his followers an easy life or a long one. Rather, he said they must take up their cross and follow him. The brightest jewel among the converts of the early church, Stephen, was stoned to death while still a young man. The church must expect to experience suffering and bereavement as a sharing with Christ in humanity's lot. We live in a world in rebellion against God where the forces of darkness and death are still at large. Nobody has been granted immunity from them.

According to this viewpoint, our question should not be, 'Why Matthew?' but 'Why not

Matthew?'—because the privilege of human freedom in a fallen world means that all of us run the real danger of 'accidental' death every day. So our focus should be on what God is doing in response to the event. After all, God's normal way of dealing with suffering is not to prevent it but to redeem it: to transform something apparently bad into something truly good; to turn apparent defeat into victory. That happened at Easter through the crucifixion and resurrection of Jesus: the supreme example of redemption—the way God works all things together for good for those who love him.

This answer, however, did not altogether satisfy us. It seemed to suggest that God is a helpless bystander in the face of tragedy—his role limited to helping any survivors; whereas Christians ask God in their prayers to direct their lives and experience that he *does* guide and over-rule. If Matthew's life had been a gift of God, how could we see his death as having nothing to do with him? Yet we couldn't think of God as *causing* Matthew's death because it was necessary to some purpose of his. That seemed like suggesting that God was the author of an evil event in order to satisfy his mysterious will. The majority of cases of infant and child deaths in the world are caused by malnutrition, poverty, poor medical facilities, ignorance, and armed conflict. Surely no one would say that God deliberately plans for such deaths.

Christine and I knew that there was no easy solution. We had problems with settling for either the 'human freedom' or the 'God's will' approach. Instead, we felt that we needed to hold on to them both. Matthew's death was, at one level, an accident. Yet God had been with us at the time and could have prevented it. But for some good reason he hadn't done so. In accepting this paradox, we acknowledged our very partial knowledge of a God much greater than us—and found peace.

But that didn't stop us asking 'Why?' It would have been tempting to run away from that question on the grounds that we could never hope to find a completely satisfying answer; that God's ways are higher than our ways so we just have to look for what he is doing in the present; that we could torture ourselves endlessly by clutching at straw after straw for answers that never quite bore the weight of the initial event. But we did not want to bury the question in despair simply because it was hard or because complete answers were not forthcoming. Nor did we want to have to answer Ruth with a simple, 'Don't know.' When Jesus was on the cross he cried out, 'My God my God, why?' If *he* needed to ask, 'Why?', so did we. All our experience of God was that he was a gracious Father who, in his own way and time, answers our urgent and important questions. We decided that we must have the courage to ask him the question 'Why?' head on, and listen for, as well as work out, his answer to it.

We reviewed again our warnings and premonitions: Matthew's last Explorer lesson with Christine, and the other 'coincidences' which had suggested God's hand in events. We remembered how God had spoken to Ruth in Innsbruck: 'I love Matthew more than you do and I want him to be with me now.' All this helped us to accept that it was within God's will for Matthew to die; that, in the end, from a heavenly perspective, it was right and good that his life had lasted for so short a time. So we changed our question from 'Why did you allow Matthew to be killed?' to 'Why did you give us the gift of Matthew for those ten years?'

Each day during Holy Week, our curate's wife, Tracy Bowsher, ran a children's drama club at church. The culmination was the Good Friday Family Service. During the service the children put together the pieces of a giant jigsaw puzzle containing scenes from the story of Holy Week. Afterwards, each child took home a jigsaw—with the central piece missing—and was asked to complete the jigsaw by returning on Easter Sunday to collect the missing piece.

We felt that the problem of Matthew's death was rather like a jigsaw with the central piece missing. God had given us a bundle of pieces. We could fit them together and make some sort of picture. True, we would probably have to wait for our own day of resurrection to receive the central piece; only then, in God's presence with Matthew, would all become clear to us. Meantime, we could go round with our bag of jigsaw pieces, moaning that there was one piece missing; or we could do the best we could with the pieces we had.

We felt that there were six crucial pieces which gave us quite a good idea of what the completed picture might look like.

The first was our understanding of heaven as a place of achievement and fulfilment. This removed any idea about Matthew's brief life on earth being wasted or pointless. We felt that we had completed our job with him; that he had achieved what God had wanted him to on earth; and that now he was in heaven, achieving what God wanted him to achieve there.

One of Matthew's best friends, Jonathan, had been, initially, very angry with God for letting Matthew die. Later, when he had calmed down, he'd said to his Mum, 'I don't know why I was so angry with God, if Matthew's gone to heaven. I know it's where Matthew always wanted to go because he kept on talking about it.' We, too, felt that the purpose of Matthew's life had been to prepare him for heaven, and that God had given him to us so that we could play our part in that preparation.

The second 'piece' was our knowledge that our own grief and suffering were not pointless. The gift of Matthew had been changing us for good when we had been enjoying that gift, and was continuing to change us for good now that it had been taken away from us. He had given to us more than we had given to him and his death had enriched Christine, Ruth and me so that we could begin to live more effectively in God's world. We were being healed not only in the sense of being restored to where we were before, but also in the sense of finding a new peace and wholeness. Suffering doesn't automatically bring entry into the fellowship of Christ's sufferings, but we felt that we had been granted that entry through the temporary gift of Matthew; granted the solemn privilege of taking up our crosses and following Jesus. Our very struggle with the question 'Why?' had itself deepened our relationship with God.

The third 'piece' was realising that Matthew
had been spared the suffering that life inevitably
brings. He had been given to us until he had been
shaped and formed enough for his future in
heaven. For all we knew, his earthly future might
have been hard, and certainly it would not have
been a patch on his heavenly life.

The fourth 'piece' was the effect of
Matthew's life and death on others. A few, like Iain
Armstrong, had come to faith directly through it.
The gift of Matthew had led him to the gift of
eternal life, whereby God and Iain would enjoy one
another's company for eternity. Others had
experienced enriched faith and deeper commitment to Christ through the loss of Matthew. Also,
we believed, God would touch others through the
book I was writing.

The fifth 'piece' was connected with India.
Through Matthew's death and the church's
response to it, there was a greater chance of life for
the boys at Pauline Bhavan. My visit there would,
perhaps, be only the start of our link with them.

The jigsaw was not complete and we felt that
God would continue adding 'pieces' as time went
by. However, the sixth crucial 'piece' related to our
expected baby.

14
Easter joy

It was apparent that we had not been very clear-thinking in our family planning. On the one hand we had been more than happy with our two delightful children. On the other hand, we had always felt that we would outlive Matthew; so why had we not thought ahead and tried to have a third child who would always be there to grow up with Ruth? Seeing Ruth's terrible loneliness without Matthew in the months following his death re-inforced our regret about not having thought things through properly. On the other hand, we felt that God's timing for the baby might be 'now' rather than earlier. There was still time to think about having another child as Ruth had asked in Innsbruck—Christine being thirty-six and myself thirty-seven.

We prayed at length about the matter. The idea that Matthew's death could lead to the coming into being of a new life seemed appropriate and appealed to us very much. It would further help to answer the question of why we had been given

Matthew for so short a time. But starting a family again after so many years was a daunting prospect.

However, a few weeks after Matthew's death, we began to try to have another child. People are usually advised (and often rightly) not to make any big decisions too soon after bereavement. But, because we were so sure that trying for another baby was right and because of our age, we didn't stick to that 'rule'. Also, we felt that God was using our family circumstances to speak to others. He had done this in the past with others, including the prophets Isaiah and Hosea. A verse from Isaiah particularly struck Christine in her daily Bible readings at this time:

> Here am I, and the children the Lord has given me. We are signs and symbols in Israel from the Lord Almighty (Isaiah 8:18).

Just as Hosea's children had symbolic names, so, we realised, did ours. Matthew was our Gift of God. Ruth, in the Old Testament story, was the person who stayed for ever with Naomi after the death of her son: a tower of strength in bereavement and the hope for the future—just like our Ruth. Now we were thinking about the possibility of a third child.

One day in Innsbruck Christine had confided in me that if we ever did have another son, she would like to call him Joseph: my father's, grandfather's and great-grandfather's first name. She felt that doing this would help my father in his grieving and continue a family tradition. Also, the name Joseph means, 'The Lord has added,' and we would certainly need the Lord's help if Christine were to conceive so close to the trauma of Matthew's death.

I teased her gently about being slightly premature with a name, but added that the same day on which she had thought of 'Joseph', the name 'Barnabas' had come forcibly to me! Its meaning, 'Son of Encouragement', seemed appropriate, since a new son would certainly be an encouragement to us, just as Barnabas, the New Testament Christian leader, had been to Paul and others. Only later did we remember with interest that Barnabas had been given his name after he had become a Christian and that his original name had been Joseph.

So we decided that if we had a son we would call him Joseph Barnabas—'The Lord has added a son of encouragement.'

During the early weeks back in England, Christine's daily Bible readings seemed to be full of promises about children!

The people walking in darkness have seen a great light; on those living in the land of the shadow of death a light has dawned ... For to us a child is born, to us a son is given (Isaiah 9:2).

This verse, the great promise to Israel of a Messiah, came to her as God's promise of another son in her bereavement.

On the second day after Matthew's funeral, I was scheduled to preach on the story of God asking Abraham to sacrifice his only son, Isaac. This seemed too much for us all to bear and so I changed to the story of God's initial promise to Abraham that he would have a son (Genesis

15:1–6). As I preached, I felt that God was making a similar promise to me.

A few weeks later, however, I awoke full of fears and doubts about the future. Would I really be given another son or see any of the good things for which we were hoping? But in the days that followed, God seemed to reassure me through Bible verses and I decided to keep trusting him, no matter how I felt.

As Christine and I continued to compare notes about the promises we felt we had received about a child, or, more precisely, a son, we wondered also about how, apart from his name, he could be a sign and symbol from the Lord.

'What if he were to be born on Easter Sunday?' asked Christine, one day.

'Yes, the day of resurrection!' I replied, 'That would be quite something.'

In mid-August we went to a Church Youth Fellowship Association (CYFA) camp at Criccieth in North Wales, taking with us a group of teenagers from St Mark's. We had wondered, in view of Matthew's death, whether to change our arrangement, but Ruth had settled the matter for us. She had very much wanted to go and had assured us that she would be all right since we had never planned to have Matthew with us: he had been scheduled to go instead with a friend to a Crusader camp nearby.

It was as we were packing that Christine began to suspect that she might be pregnant. A day or two later, at camp, she acquired a pregnancy home-testing kit. It was quite tricky operating this in a camp toilet but the result was clear. My wife was certainly pregnant! And, according to her calculations, the baby had been conceived very soon after we had decided to try for another child. In the circumstances of the trauma we had gone through, this was, we felt, quite amazing. Looking ahead, we calculated that the baby would be due on April 19th—Easter Sunday of the following year!

As the months passed, the promised baby became increasingly important to us as a sign of hope for the future. It was especially important to Ruth not to reach her next birthday without a brother or sister and this wish looked like being granted since the baby was due a month before her ninth birthday. However, the importance of the baby to all three of us meant that we also had to contend with fears about miscarriage and handicap. These were heightened by our recent loss experience. But we determined to have no amniocentesis or other test for handicap: this child was from God and there was no circumstance in which we would have countenanced a termination. Our doubts and fears were not about God's ability to deliver what he seemed to have promised to us. Rather they stemmed from a periodic loss of confidence in our own ability to interpret properly what God was saying. The fact that we very much wanted a baby boy made us wonder at times whether we were indulging in wishful thinking.

Naturally, Christine longed for a perfectly healthy baby. But she felt that she just had to trust God to give her the grace to cope if the child were handicapped in any way.

Christine kept remarkably fit and healthy, and the baby seemed to develop without causing us any alarms or worries. It seemed to register its presence at all the right moments, having an early kicking session on November 5th when Christine, in tears, was remembering the making of Matthew's birthday cake the year before—as though reminding her that there would be many other birthday cakes.

During the tense and busy period before Christmas I was writing in the study when Ruth came in—her eyes shining.

'I've just felt the baby move, Dad,' she said. 'I put my hand on Mum's tum and felt it kick me.'

'I'm very pleased you've felt it, Ruth,' I said. 'I've seen its picture on the scan at the hospital and now the baby is real to both of us.'

It was because of the baby that I had gone alone to India. Fulwood church had generously offered to pay all three of our air fares, but our doctor had advised Christine not to risk the trip, so it had been decided that she and Ruth would stay at home. Though disappointed, they had been happy for me to go without them—though we had agreed that one day we would all travel there together.

And so the months went by as we put together our new life and prepared for the baby. As the delivery date approached the tension and excitement mounted. Would everything be all right? Were we right in expecting a boy? When would the baby arrive?

'You won't have the baby this week,' said the midwife to Christine at the Tuesday clinic in Holy Week. 'You are still putting on weight.' Christine wasn't so sure. The following day she felt things beginning to move and I stayed close at hand,

cancelling a radio interview which would have
involved me travelling some miles away in the
afternoon. After the evening service at St Mark's, I
returned home just in time for our regular house-
group. After the group had gone, at about 10.30
p.m. the first major contractions began.

'Let's go to bed: they might stop and we
could get some sleep,' I counselled. Ten minutes
was all we got before it was obvious that we had to
dress and take Ruth to friends living just round the
corner—Rosie and George Clark. Christine and I
arrived at 11.15 p.m. at Northern General
Hospital, where I had been born thirty-seven years
earlier. The contractions were now getting more
fierce and soon things started happening. I sat by
Christine's bed and held her hand.

The baby's head appeared first. Outwardly
calm, I was finding the suspense hard to contain. I
watched keenly as the rest of the little body was
born and listened to the baby's first hesitant noises.

'What is it?' whispered Christine, hardly
daring to ask.

'You have a son,' I replied, my heart burst-
ing.

'No!' she said, afraid to believe it.

'Oh, yes you have!' I assured her, grinning
as I moved round to take our son from the
midwife. He was still bloody but very beautiful.
The Lord had added our son of encouragement. It
was one o'clock on Maundy Thursday morning,
the day that Jesus had agonised in the Garden of
Gethsemane and bent his will to his Father's—
accepting suffering and death; the day that suffering and resurrection were decided upon as the way

of salvation for mankind.

The doctor on duty was a friend and fellow-Christian from Fulwood—Jo Hopkins. She rejoiced with us, then told Christine that she needed a few stitches, adding that Ruth could come and see us first if we liked.

I went to the phone and rang Rosie. Ruth came on the phone but was unable even to say 'hello' in the tension of the moment.

'You have a brother, my darling,' I told her. 'Ask Aunty Rosie to bring you down.'

'That's wonderful,' whispered Ruth in a small, choked voice. I then rang Christine's and my parents—full of joy that I was able, on this occasion, to phone them with good news.

'It's a miracle,' said my Mum repeatedly. I knew that the excitement would mean a sleepless night for her as well.

Ruth arrived soon and was able to hold Joseph—before he was an hour old—in her arms.

'He's beautiful,' she said in awe and with deep pleasure. It was a very special moment. Then Rosie took Ruth back to bed, and, while Christine was being stitched, I was able to enjoy some time with my son.

He had arrived at just the right time—better even than if he had come on Easter Sunday itself: his earlier arrival meant that the whole of Easter could be the time of resurrection for our family life.

Very soon, Christine and Joseph were both pronounced fit and well. They came home on Saturday. So Easter Sunday was our first full day together as a new family. The Lord's timing, as always, had been perfect.

Everyone at St Mark's had mourned for Matthew with us, and had followed the pregnancy closely. Now on Easter Sunday they could celebrate with us. The church was fuller for the Family Service than it had been at any time since Matthew's funeral; extra chairs had to be brought in.

We began with the time-honoured response: 'Alleluia! Christ is risen: He is risen indeed. Alleluia!' We repeated the response three times, rising to a great crescendo of sound in honour of the risen Lord.

After the service, Christine brought Joseph down to the church hall where he was introduced to the congregation and the celebrations continued. God had added a son of encouragement, not just for us but for the whole church.

And so, with the celebrations of Easter's resurrection ringing in our ears, we finish our story. There is as yet no more to tell. As I write, it is Easter Sunday afternoon, ten months after Matthew's death and three days after Joseph's birth. The future, as always, is unknown. But we have unshakeable confidence in the God of resurrection glory, and place the future of our new family in his hands. And one great day, when our family is finally together, when each of us will have joined Matthew in the eternal company of heaven, the celebration proper will begin, to continue throughout eternity.

WILLIAM'S STORY

Rosemary Attlee

A mother's account of her son's struggle
against cancer

'A story that glints with honesty, anguish
and love. What redeems the tragedy in
the end is faith, for in losing his life
William truly finds it.'

Luci Shaw

'A testimony to the amazing grace of
God'

Bishop Morris Maddocks

The paradox of a loving God and
suffering man resolved in the acceptance
of a loving and heavenly Father.

HIGHLAND BOOKS